THE PLANTATION
SOUTH

THE PLANTATION
SOUTH
1934–1937

by
William C. Holley
Ellen Winston
T. J. Woofter, Jr.

BOOKS FOR LIBRARIES PRESS
FREEPORT, NEW YORK

First Published 1940
Reprinted 1971

INTERNATIONAL STANDARD BOOK NUMBER:
0-8369-5844-6

LIBRARY OF CONGRESS CATALOG CARD NUMBER:
74-160977

PRINTED IN THE UNITED STATES OF AMERICA

Contents

	Page
Introduction	XI
Summary	XV
Chapter I. Changes in plantation organization and operation	1
Land organization	3
Organization of cropland	5
Organization of cropland by tenure	7
Cotton yield	9
Plantation livestock	10
Chapter II. Changes in plantation labor and power	13
Labor	13
Predominance of Negro labor	15
Utilization of off-plantation labor	15
Type of off-plantation labor	16
Transportation	17
Changes in power	17
Prospects for increased mechanization	20
Chapter III. Credit	23
Operators' long-term indebtedness	23
Operators' short-term credit	24
Tenants' short-term credit	26
Chapter IV. Plantation income	29
Investment per plantation	29
Gross plantation income	30
Current expenses	34
Plantation net cash income	3€

Page

Chapter V. Operator and tenant income _ _ _ _ _ _ _ _ _ _ _ _ 39

    Operator's cash income _ _ _ _ _ _ _ _ _ _ _ _ _ 39

        Gross cash income_ _ _ _ _ _ _ _ _ _ _ _ _ _ _ 39

        Current expenses _ _ _ _ _ _ _ _ _ _ _ _ _ _ 40

        Net cash income _ _ _ _ _ _ _ _ _ _ _ _ _ _ _ 41

        Net cash gain or loss _ _ _ _ _ _ _ _ _ _ _ _ 41

    Tenant's cash income _ _ _ _ _ _ _ _ _ _ _ _ _ _ 43

        Gross cash income_ _ _ _ _ _ _ _ _ _ _ _ _ _ _ 43

        Current expenses _ _ _ _ _ _ _ _ _ _ _ _ _ _ 44

        Net cash income _ _ _ _ _ _ _ _ _ _ _ _ _ _ 45

            Net cash income by cotton acreage _ _ _ _ _ _ 45

        Net income_ _ _ _ _ _ _ _ _ _ _ _ _ _ _ _ _ _ 46

Chapter VI. Relief needs in the South _ _ _ _ _ _ _ _ _ _ _ 47

    Population trends_ _ _ _ _ _ _ _ _ _ _ _ _ _ _ _ 48

    Change in number of farm operators, 1930 to 1935 _ _ _ 48

    Extent of Federal aid _ _ _ _ _ _ _ _ _ _ _ _ _ _ _ 51

Chapter VII. Living conditions _ _ _ _ _ _ _ _ _ _ _ _ _ 55

    Diet_ 55

    Housing _ _ _ _ _ _ _ _ _ _ _ _ _ _ _ _ _ _ _ 58

    Health_ _ _ _ _ _ _ _ _ _ _ _ _ _ _ _ _ _ _ 60

    Education _ _ _ _ _ _ _ _ _ _ _ _ _ _ _ _ _ _ _ 63

    Plane of living _ _ _ _ _ _ _ _ _ _ _ _ _ _ _ _ 67

Chapter VIII. Programs and policies _ _ _ _ _ _ _ _ _ 71

Appendix A. Supplementary tables _ _ _ _ _ _ _ _ _ 79

Appendix B. List of tables _ _ _ _ _ _ _ _ _ _ _ _ 99

Appendix C. Method and scope of the study _ _ _ _ _ _ _ 103

Appendix D. Changes in labor requirements for cotton production_ 115

Index _ 119

ILLUSTRATIONS

Figures

Figure	Page
1. Plantations enumerated, 1937 and 1934 _ _ _ _ _ _ _ _ _	XII
2. Areas included in survey _ _ _ _ _ _ _ _ _ _ _ _ _ _ _	XIII
3. Operation of crop acres per plantation, by tenure, 1937 and 1934 _	7
4. Organization of cropland per plantation, by tenure, 1937 and 1934 _	9
5. Resident families per plantation, by type, 1937 and 1934 _	14
6. Tractors per plantation, 1937 _ _ _ _ _ _ _ _ _ _ _ _ _	19
7. Gross income from cash receipts per plantation, by area, 1937 and 1934 _ _ _ _ _ _ _ _ _ _ _ _ _ _ _ _ _ _ _	32
8. Net cash income per plantation, by area, 1937 and 1934 _	36
9. Cash income per operator, by area, 1937 and 1934 _ _ _ _	42
10. Federal aid per capita, January 1933–March 1938 _ _ _ _	52
11. Rural-farm plane-of-living index in 32 rural-farm cultural regions, 1930 _	67

Photographs

Plantation owner's dwelling _ _ _ _ _ _ _ _ _ _ _	Facing	XIV
Plantation buildings _ _ _ _ _ _ _ _ _ _ _ _ _ _ _	Facing	XXII
Cotton choppers with riding boss_ _ _ _ _ _ _ _ _	Facing	4
Hoe work _	Facing	12
One-half row cotton cultivation _ _ _ _ _ _ _ _ _	Facing	16
One-row cotton cultivation _ _ _ _ _ _ _ _ _ _ _	Facing	18
Four-row cotton cultivation _ _ _ _ _ _ _ _ _ _ _	Facing	22
Collecting cotton pickers _ _ _ _ _ _ _ _ _ _ _ _	Facing	26
Pickers at work _ _ , _ _ _ _ _ _ _ _ _ _ _ _ _ _	Facing	32
Weighing up_ _ _ _ _ _ _ _ _ _ _ _ _ _ _ _ _ _ _	Facing	36
Loading for the gin_ _ _ _ _ _ _ _ _ _ _ _ _ _ _ _	Facing	42
Mechanical cotton picker at work _ _ _ _ _ _ _ _	Facing	46
Sharecropper home_ _ _ _ _ _ _ _ _ _ _ _ _ _ _ _	Facing	58

The Plantation South, 1934–1937

IX

INTRODUCTION

WITHIN RECENT years changes in plantation organization and operation have been proceeding at a rapid rate in the South-eastern States. In order to provide a definitive answer concerning some of the causes of economic insecurity and labor displacement in plantation areas of the Southeast, it appeared desirable to repeat the plantation survey analyzed in the report *Landlord and Tenant on the Cotton Plantation*.[1] The earlier survey covers plantation operations for the crop year 1934 while the resurvey is based on farm operations in 1937 and the current situation at the time of the field survey in the summer of 1938. To the extent that the schedule was expanded for the resurvey, the emphasis was placed on changes in the labor force and in the use of machinery. The crop year 1937 was exceptional as the crop control program was on a voluntary basis, resulting in an unusually large cotton acreage, and as climatic conditions were especially favorable for cotton production. The implications of these factors are of basic significance in any comparison of the data for 1934 and 1937.

A total of 246 schedules was secured in the survey of the 1937 crop year which could be matched with schedules for the same plantations from the 1934 enumeration (table 1 and fig. 1).[2] For the earlier survey a plantation was defined as a tract with five or more resident families, including the landlord, and this definition was retained in the later study.

The plantations included in the present survey fall into nine areas,[3] two fewer than were covered by the more extensive study made as of 1934.[4] The Atlantic Coast Plain Area includes the general cotton-

---

[1] Woofter, T. J., Jr. and Others, Research Monograph V, Division of Social Research, Works Progress Administration, Washington, D. C., 1936.

[2] See Appendix C, Method and Scope of the Study.

[3] These areas do not coincide with the type-of-farming areas delineated by the Bureau of Agricultural Economics, U. S. Department of Agriculture.

[4] The Upper Piedmont and Muscle Shoals Areas were included in the 1934 survey.

Table 1.—Plantations Enumerated, by Area, 1937 and 1934

Area	Plantations enumerated	
	Number	Percent
All areas	246	100. 0
Atlantic Coast Plain	31	12. 6
Black Belt (A)	31	12. 6
Black Belt (B)	16	6. 5
Upper Delta	79	32. 1
Lower Delta	19	7. 7
Interior Plain	17	6. 9
Mississippi Bluffs	27	11. 0
Red River	15	6. 1
Arkansas River	11	4. 5

tobacco area of the eastern part of North and South Carolina and of eastern and southeastern Georgia (fig. 2). West of this area, extending southwest from North Carolina through South Carolina and Georgia and crossing central Alabama and extending into east central Mississippi, is the Black Belt, the traditional plantation area. This in turn has been divided into two segments: (A) the area in which croppers and other share tenants constituted a majority of all tenants in 1930, and (B) the area in which renters constituted a majority in 1930.

Fig. I – PLANTATIONS ENUMERATED
1937 and 1934

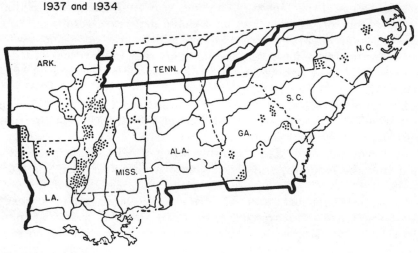

Each dot represents one plantation.

WPA 3304

The Delta Area, divided into an upper and a lower section for purposes of analysis, follows both banks of the Mississippi River and extends part way up its tributaries—the Red, the Yazoo, and the Arkansas. To the east of this area, extending from southern

Fig. 2 — AREAS INCLUDED IN SURVEY

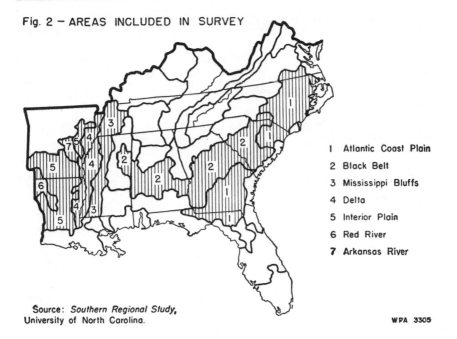

1　Atlantic Coast Plain

2　Black Belt

3　Mississippi Bluffs

4　Delta

5　Interior Plain

6　Red River

7　Arkansas River

Source: *Southern Regional Study,*
University of North Carolina.

WPA 3305

Mississippi northward through Tennessee, lies the Mississippi Bluffs Area. To the west is the Interior Plain of southern Arkansas and central and northern Louisiana. Smaller areas are formed by the bottom lands along the Red River and the Arkansas River.

The study samples the larger agricultural units within these areas, and hence its findings are applicable to plantation organization rather than descriptive of the agriculture of the Southeast in general. That the smaller operating units were affected by the same factors as the larger holdings during the period covered in the study is undoubtedly true, but the data at hand are inadequate as a basis for generalizing concerning those units.

Such a study of changes occurring in plantation organization and operation is particularly needed because of the generally low level of living among the agricultural population throughout the South and the persistence of the need for relief which far exceeds available facilities for alleviating distress. Moreover, in view of present agricultural trends and the pressure of population on economic opportunity resulting in widespread unemployment and underemployment, the situation exhibits many characteristics which will not change to any marked extent within the near future.

Plantation Owner's Dwelling.

SUMMARY

RAPID AND significant agricultural changes have been occurring in the Cotton Belt within recent years. On the cotton plantation the general tendency, as shown by surveys in 1934 and 1937, has been in the direction of slightly larger units. For all areas combined the size of plantations surveyed increased during the 3-year period from an average of 955 acres to 1,014 acres. Coincident with this expansion was an increase in the number of acres devoted to crops. The largest proportion of plantations had from 200 to 400 acres in crops in both years, but an increase occurred during the period of survey in the number of plantations with very large crop acreages. The average acreage in woodland also rose. Conversely, the acreages in idle cropland and in farmsteads, roads, ditches, and wasteland declined.

With the exception of the Black Belt (A) Area, all nine areas surveyed had from 30 to 60 percent of the crop acreage planted to cotton in both 1934 and 1937. The fact that the crop control program was on a voluntary basis in 1937 accounted for a significant increase in the proportion of the total cropland in cotton in comparison with the earlier year. Corn was planted on practically all plantations and ranked second in crop acreage.

Not only was there an increase in cotton acreage but also the average yield rose from 268 pounds of lint cotton per acre in 1934 for all areas combined to 456 pounds in 1937. A variety of factors, such as more favorable climatic conditions, improved seed, increased use of commercial fertilizer, larger acreages in leguminous crops in 1936, inducements provided by the soil conservation program of the Agricultural Adjustment Administration, decreased damage from plant disease and insect infestation, and developments in methods of production, affected this increase.

Coincident with the increase in crop acreage was the increase in the average number of work stock owned by the plantation operator. The number of cows also increased while the expansion in the number of pigs was even more important. Even with such trends, however, the number of livestock per plantation tended to remain relatively small.

A major consideration affecting the plantation operator's organization and operation plans is the relative availability and economy of the various types of labor. The slight increase from 15 to 16 resident families per plantation in all areas from 1934 to 1937 was due to increases in cropland and especially in cropland planted to cotton. This resulted in increased requirements for hand labor. However, the average number of resident families per 1,000 acres of cropland decreased from almost 37 to 34 during the period studied.

Croppers were the most important type of plantation labor, operating approximately 46 percent of all cropland in both years. Wage laborers were the second most important source of labor and, for all areas combined, operated 41 percent of the cropland in 1937 as compared with 36 percent in 1934. Renters declined markedly from 1934 to 1937 in terms of number of families per 1,000 acres of cropland, and croppers and share tenants decreased slightly. Only wage laborers held their own.

Negro families were dominant on the plantations surveyed, outnumbering white families by approximately 9 to 1. Few plantations were operated solely by white tenants.

There was wide variation from area to area in the use of off-plantation labor for cotton chopping and picking, both local and migratory labor being utilized. Operators usually provided the transportation for the latter group. Migratory laborers for cotton picking were recruited an average distance of 79 miles from the plantations on which they were employed.

An increase in the average number of work stock per plantation between 1934 and 1937 was reported for all areas. In most areas, however, the number of work stock per 1,000 acres of cropland remained about stationary. At the same time increases in the number of tractors per 1,000 acres of cropland were reported in all areas except the Lower Delta, Interior Plain, and Arkansas River Areas. This increase in mechanization was directly associated with the increase in the proportion of total cropland and of cotton acreage operated with wage labor. On 131 of the 246 plantations power was provided by both work stock and tractors, and 2 plantations were entirely mechanized. Almost half of the plantations with tractors had only one. Mechanization is retarded by such factors as lack of available capital at a low rate of interest, need for an adequate supply of labor during peak seasons, unsuitable land, and preference for work stock or sufficient numbers of work stock on hand for plantation operation.

Cotton, more than any other major crop, has resisted the general trend toward mechanization in agriculture. Although an increase in the use of various laborsaving devices may be expected, the rate of adoption in the areas surveyed will be gradual. In many cases it will continue to be economically advantageous to insure an adequate supply of harvest labor by employing the laborers throughout the year.

A plantation is a business enterprise with the operator using long-term credit to provide capital assets and short-term credit to meet current operating expenses. Long-term debts, which usually are secured by real-estate mortgages, were reported by a smaller proportion of the plantations in 1937 than in 1934. There was a definite trend toward an increase in Government loans as compared with other types, and the rate of interest declined during the period for mortgages held by both governmental and nongovernmental agencies. As a result of larger plantation profits operators had been enabled to reduce their long-term indebtedness from an average of $13,018 to $11,914. While mortgages remained by far the most important type of long-term indebtedness, they were of less importance relatively in 1937 than in 1934, because improved financial circumstances made it possible for operators to repay some of their obligations, thus opening up new credit channels.

In order to provide short-term credit for financing his own operations and making necessary advances to his tenants, the plantation operator usually gives a first lien on the cash crops under cultivation and often additional liens on livestock and implements. Banks are still the principal source of such loans although they have been decreasing somewhat in importance, particularly because of the increased facilities offered by Government agencies. Merchant loans have also decreased in importance.

Interest rates are high on short-term loans because a per annum rate is normally charged, although the loan is usually for only a few months. Thus, even on Government loans, which were secured on more favorable terms than loans from other sources, operators paid a rate of almost 12 percent per annum in both 1937 and 1934.

Croppers and share tenants are ordinarily dependent on credit from the landlord to cover costs of production and subsistence. As security the operator takes liens on their cash crops and such farm equipment as they may possess. On the plantations surveyed, subsistence advances were made for 7 months on the average and increased slightly from $13.70 per month in 1934 to $14.50 in 1937. Although operators themselves pay high interest charges for short-term credit, rates for tenants are two to three times as high, averaging 36 percent on an annual basis in 1937. Such heavy charges increase the difficulties of the tenant in rising to a higher tenure status and operate against diversification of crops because the tenant must concentrate on the cash crop in order to meet his obligations.

The financial operations involved in plantation management are complicated by the variety of activities engaged in, which normally expand as the size of the unit and number of resident families increase.

The total investment usually represents a rather heavy capital outlay. For all areas the investment per plantation at conservative market values increased from $31,378 in 1934 to $37,504 in 1937. Almost three-fourths of the total was accounted for by land. Investment per crop acre also rose during the same period.

As obtained in the survey, data on plantation gross income included current cash receipts from farming operations only, including AAA payments. Financial returns from plantation-operated nonfarm enterprises were not reported. Crop sales accounted for approximately 85 percent of the gross cash receipts for both years, and AAA benefits were second in importance. Other sources of income were sale of livestock products, interest on advances to tenants, cash rent from land, commissions through resale of farm products, and returns from special work performed by the operator or under his supervision. In only one area, the Atlantic Coast Plain, did the sale of lint cotton and cottonseed amount to less than 50 percent of the total cash receipts. Both AAA cash benefits and sale of livestock products increased in total amount during the period of the study. The wide variation in gross cash income is revealed by the fact that the gross income per plantation for the one-fourth of the units with the highest incomes was more than double the average for all plantations in both 1937 and 1934.

Current expenses per plantation also increased during the period studied. Wages paid to laborers, the most important single item, rose from 31 percent of the total expenditures in 1934 to 36 percent in 1937 as a result of expanded cotton acreage and the high yields in 1937 as compared with 1934. Current expenses deducted from gross plantation income to give net income included, in addition to labor expenses, expenditures for feed, seed, and fertilizer; interest on short-term loans; costs of current repairs to plantation buildings, fences, and implements; insurance and taxes; and miscellaneous items. On the average, the net cash income per plantation increased from $5,689 in 1934 to $7,673 in 1937. Factors responsible for this rise included increased crop acreage planted to cotton and exceptionally high yields.

From the point of view of both operator and tenant the success of the year's plantation operations is determined primarily by the net cash income received. The gross income of the operator is dependent to a large extent on the total acreage in crops, the proportion planted to cotton, the average yield per acre, and the price level of the money crop. Deducting current expenses from gross cash income, the average operator received a net cash income of $3,590 in 1937 as compared with $2,528 in 1934. Only the three most eastern areas surveyed failed to show increases.

The operator's net cash income, however, represents the return for his supervisory labor and interest on his invested capital. Deducting a 6 percent return on invested capital, operator labor income was $1,340 in 1937 as compared with $645 in 1934.

Less than 10 percent of the total operators in either year reported actual losses in their plantation enterprises, and most of the losses amounted to less than $500. In contrast, 27 percent of all operators received $5,000 or more in 1937 and averaged net cash incomes of $10,268 as compared with 15 percent and an average income of $9,362 for 1934. Moreover, all the data point to the fact that the plantation operator was in a much sounder position financially in 1937 than in 1934.

The gross cash income of croppers and share tenants resulting from crop sales, AAA payments, and plantation occasional labor for wages averaged $385 in 1937 as compared with $331 in 1934. Cotton was the main source of this income in all areas except the Atlantic Coast Plain Area where tobacco accounted for approximately one-half of the crop sales.

After deducting expenses for actual crop production, the net income of croppers and share tenants combined rose from $263 in 1934 to $300 in 1937. Of these totals $112 was for subsistence advances and $151 for net cash income after settling in 1934 and $104 for subsistence advances and $196 for net cash income in 1937. On the basis of these low net incomes which, even when production for home use was added to them, averaged only about $400 in the good cotton year of 1937, the average Southern tenant can neither maintain an acceptable level of living nor look forward to raising his tenure status.

The principal changes occurring in the cotton plantation organization, operation, and income between 1934 and 1937 may be summarized as follows:

Principal Changes in Plantation Organization, Operation, and Income, 1934–1937

Item	1937	1934	Change	
			Actual	Percent
Total acres	1,014	955	+59	+6
Crop acres	477	417	+60	+14
Cotton acres	230	178	+52	+29
Livestock: [1]				
Mules and horses	20	16	+4	+25
Cows	28	16	+12	+75
Pigs	31	16	+15	+94
Work stock per 1,000 acres in crops	48	47	+1	+2
Tractors per 1,000 acres in crops	2.3	1.8	+0.5	+28
Resident families per 1,000 acres in crops	34	37	−3	−8
Mortgage debt, percent reporting	41	52	−11	−21
Size of mortgage debt	$11,914	$13,018	−$1,104	−9
Net cash income per operator	$3,590	$2,528	+$1,062	+42
Net income [2] per tenant [3]	$300	$263	+$37	+14
Cash	$196	$151	+$45	+30
Subsistence advances	$104	$112	−$8	−7

[1] Excludes livestock owned by tenants.
[2] Excludes home-use production which was estimated at approximately $100.
[3] Includes croppers and share tenants only.

Problems arising in connection with changes in agricultural income, with increased mechanization, and with variations in labor requirements are directly associated with relief needs in the South. Because such needs are widespread throughout the rural South, the problem has been analyzed for the section as a whole rather than for the more limited area in which cotton production dominates. More than one-half of the farm population of the Nation is in the South, and the basic causes of Southern relief problems are to be found in the maladjustments of this farm population in relation to agricultural opportunity and its pressure toward the towns and villages where it cannot be absorbed. Population has backed up steadily on the farms in recent years as a result of decreased urbanward migration, and the pressure of persons of working age has become more and more serious. Population increases in the South from 1930 to 1935 occurred primarily outside of the major cotton regions, where both the total farm population and the number of farm operators were approximately the same on April 1, 1930, and January 1, 1935. Owners and tenants in the cotton regions increased somewhat but croppers declined by nearly 10 percent. Data from the Unemployment Census of November 1937 substantiate the fact that unemployment of farm operators and farm laborers is more widespread in the South than in the country as a whole. Extensive need, present at all times, becomes especially acute during the winter months when the low-income farmer has neither adequate funds to tide him over until the new crop year nor available sources of between-season employment.

On a per capita basis the South has not received as much Federal aid as most other sections. Low standards of living have led to rigorous standards of acceptance for relief and small relief benefits per case. Relief loads have varied considerably from year to year as a result of administrative factors and limitation of funds as well as of changes in the general economic situation. Of the more than 1,000,000 rural cases aided in the South in November 1938 under general relief, Works Progress Administration, and Farm Security Administration programs combined, it is estimated that about 600,000 included employable workers with farm backgrounds. Since large numbers applying for aid could not be employed by the WPA, it is obvious that the magnitude of the rural relief problem in the South is far greater than the data on case loads indicate.

In the rural South both those on relief and their nonrelief neighbors are disadvantaged with respect to living conditions and community institutions. Inadequate nutrition constitutes a basic problem in the South. Because of low incomes the adequacy of the diet is directly dependent upon production for home use. Increased emphasis on such production in turn has been found to be one step toward raising the net incomes of poverty-stricken farm families.

The dietary inadequacies of the agricultural families at the bottom of the economic ladder in the Southern States are accompanied by poor housing. On the average the Southern farm house is old and unpainted, without bathroom or basement, and one story in height. It lacks running water and in one out of three cases the roof, doors and windows, and interior walls and ceilings are in poor condition.

Related to the poor housing, inadequate sanitary facilities, and meager diets of poverty-stricken Southern rural families are high rates of illness. Provisions for prevention of contagion are frequently inadequate, and death rates from such diseases as typhoid and paratyphoid fever and malaria continue to be high as compared with other areas. A major step toward the control of malaria, however, has been the recent drainage of almost 2,000,000 acres of swamps through CWA, FERA, and WPA programs. This has affected the health of 15,000,000 people. Associated with the lag in control of various diseases are the inadequate provisions for infant and maternal care and the limited hospital facilities.

The rural South is also at a disadvantage in comparison with other sections of the country in educational facilities. The handicap of inadequate education is widespread among low-income farm families throughout the South, and this handicap applies not only to the older generation but to the rising generation as well. An effective attack on the widespread problem of illiteracy has been made through the Emergency Education Program of the FERA-WPA under which from 1933 through June 1938 more than one-half million persons in both urban and rural areas of 12 Southern States were taught to read and write. Data which show that less than 1 in 4 of the white heads of households on relief in the Eastern Cotton Area in October 1935 and only 1 in 25 of the Negro heads had advanced beyond the seventh grade are indicative of the educational status of a much larger proportion of the population than that actually receiving aid. Many factors serve to keep farm children out of school in the South but peak demands for labor in the cotton fields is one important cause.

Closely related to low incomes and lack of adequate social services are the low rural-farm plane-of-living indices among Southern regions, indices on which these regions rank at the bottom for the country as a whole. One of the most promising developments for improving living conditions in the South is the expansion of electrical service, although no Southern State is yet up to the national average of 22.1 percent for farms receiving central-station service as of June 30, 1939.

The problems of rural living in the South reflect the economic situation and emphasize the need for broad programs of economic and social reconstruction. Important steps in this direction have been taken in recent years through submarginal land retirement, soil conservation, promotion of family-sized farms and farm ownership by the Farm Security Administration, the experimental promotion of cooperative farm enterprises, increased crop diversification, credit reform, tenancy reform, and the Federal work program. Much remains to be done along all of these lines, and no Federal action has yet been taken for equalizing educational, public health, and low-income housing opportunities between rural and urban areas. Increasing attention to these problems and substantial agreement as to the things which need to be done, however, make it safe to predict that over a period of time major achievements will result.

Plantation Buildings.

Chapter I

CHANGES IN PLANTATION ORGANIZATION AND OPERATION

PLANTATION ORGANIZATION and operation in the Southeast are undergoing rapid change. Variations in production practices, in prices paid and received by farmers, and in extent of participation in agricultural adjustment programs of the Federal Government have been important factors in producing such change. The data presented for 246 plantations for the crop years 1937 and 1934 are indicative of the significant trends which are occurring.

The study is based on single-unit plantations operated either by owners or by managers who exercise the authority of owners. The plantation operator, whether owner or manager, has numerous specific duties to perform and in addition often delegates certain definite duties to subordinates in the plantation organization. The duties of the operator primarily include crop planning, financing of operations, management of labor and power, supervision of cropping practices, marketing, and management of other plantation-operated enterprises.[1] The variety of the activities and the size of the enterprises call for a high degree of managerial ability for efficient plantation operation. The success with which the operator manages the varied types of activities is largely reflected in the financial outcome of the year's work.

In spite of the many and varied activities associated with plantation management, approximately 28 percent of the plantation operators included in the study reported a second occupation to which they

[1] A detailed description of managerial functions on the plantation may be found in Woofter, T. J., Jr. and Others, *Landlord and Tenant on the Cotton Plantation*, Research Monograph V, Division of Social Research, Works Progress Administration, Washington, D. C., 1936. pp. 26–33.

devoted more than one-fourth of their time (table 2).   The proportion was almost the same for all areas combined in both 1934 and 1937. To the extent that these other occupations may result in neglect of plantation operations, they lead to speculative and inefficient agricultural operations.

Table 2.—Operators With Other Occupations,[1] by Area, 1937 and 1934

Area	Total operators	Operators with other occupations	
		1937	1934
All areas	246	68	67
Atlantic Coast Plain	31	6	6
Black Belt (A)	31	12	6
Black Belt (B)	16	3	6
Upper Delta	79	27	22
Lower Delta	19	3	4
Interior Plain	17	4	7
Mississippi Bluffs	27	9	8
Red River	15	1	3
Arkansas River	11	3	5

[1] Accounting for more than one-fourth of their time.

In addition to other occupations, absentee ownership is generally regarded as a possible deterrent to efficient plantation operation. The practice of living off the plantation was slightly less frequent in 1937 than in 1934, the proportion of operators residing on their plantations having risen from 70 percent to 73 percent during the interval (table 3).   Of those operators who lived elsewhere, the great majority were within 10 miles of their plantations.   This made possible daily supervision of operations and reduced the number of plantations possibly affected by lack of operator supervision to less than 10 percent.   Even in such cases modern transportation facilities are such that ill effects from neglect by absentee operators cannot be assumed.

Table 3.—Resident and Absentee Operators, by Area, 1937 and 1934

Area	Total operators	Number of operators living on plantations		Operators living within 10 miles of plantations		Operators living more than 10 miles from plantations	
		1937	1934	1937	1934	1937	1934
All areas:							
Number	246	180	172	44	55	22	19
Percent	100.0	73.2	69.9	17.9	22.4	8.9	7.7
Atlantic Coast Plain	31	17	15	11	15	3	1
Black Belt (A)	31	20	21	9	7	2	3
Black Belt (B)	16	16	15	—	1	—	—
Upper Delta	79	60	58	10	12	9	9
Lower Delta	19	13	11	3	6	3	2
Interior Plain	17	12	13	5	4	—	—
Mississippi Bluffs	27	20	19	5	8	2	—
Red River	15	14	14	—	—	1	1
Arkansas River	11	8	6	1	2	2	3

The increased number of operators who lived on their plantations in 1937 as compared with 1934 is related to the fact that the proportion with other farms declined from 38 percent to 26 percent.[2] Consolidation of holdings was a major factor in this decrease.

LAND ORGANIZATION

The general tendency in recent years among the plantations surveyed has been in the direction of slightly larger units, resulting in part from consolidation of farms. For all areas combined the size of plantations increased from an average of 955 acres in 1934 to 1,014 acres in 1937, an increase of approximately 6 percent (table 4). All areas had small increases except the Black Belt (B) and the Arkansas River Areas where relatively slight decreases appeared.

The changes from year to year in crop acres per plantation are due largely to changes in price outlook and Agricultural Adjustment Administration crop regulations (appendix table 1). Severe reductions in acreage were imposed during the crop years 1934 and 1935 for cotton, whereas in 1936 and 1938 the program was less severe and in 1937 it was on a voluntary basis.

Between 1934 and 1937 an increase in the average plantation acreage devoted to crops occurred in all areas with the single exception of the Black Belt (B) Area. Even in this area the proportion of the total plantation acreage devoted to crops increased slightly. For all areas 47 percent of the total acreage was planted to crops in 1937 as compared with 44 percent in 1934 (table 4). In each of the years surveyed the largest proportion of plantations contained from 200 to 400 acres in crops (appendix table 2). However, about 43 percent of the plantations devoted 400 acres or more to crops in 1937 in comparison with 36 percent in 1934. The number of plantations with from 600 to 800 crop acres more than doubled from 1934 to 1937, while plantations with crop acreages of 1,000 acres or more increased by slightly more than one-third during the same period.

Normally very small acreages of cropland are left idle on plantations. A larger total acreage was idle in 1934, when cotton acreage was curtailed by the AAA in conformity with the Bankhead Cotton Act under which a tax penalty was incurred for cotton ginned in excess of a specified quota per plantation,[3] than was idle in 1937. There was wide variation from area to area, however, with the Lower Delta and Interior Plain Areas showing particularly large proportionate increases in idle cropland in 1937 (table 4).

---

[2] Data on file in the Division of Research, Work Projects Administration, Washington, D. C.

[3] For a summary of the programs of the AAA with respect to cotton see Agricultural Adjustment Administration, *Agricultural Adjustment: 1937–38*, U. S. Department of Agriculture, Washington, D. C., 1939, *passim*.

Table 4.—Organization of Land per Plantation, by Area, 1937 and 1934

Area	Total plantations	Acres per plantation											
		Total		Crops		Idle		Pasture		Woodland		Other [1]	
		1937	1934	1937	1934	1937	1934	1937	1934	1937	1934	1937	1934
All areas	246	1,014	955	477	417	43	53	145	156	291	233	58	96
Atlantic Coast Plain	31	661	581	331	243	28	53	54	29	232	200	16	56
Black Belt (A)	31	755	730	350	303	57	48	198	157	102	170	48	52
Black Belt (B)	16	540	572	243	249	18	26	70	81	190	174	19	42
Upper Delta	79	1,112	1,111	579	542	11	59	110	140	366	284	46	86
Lower Delta	19	1,922	1,598	373	249	214	83	494	558	641	456	200	252
Interior Plain	17	770	671	397	340	57	14	110	134	186	136	20	47
Mississippi Bluffs	27	912	898	434	392	29	46	67	101	330	234	52	125
Red River	15	1,227	978	718	535	58	63	159	213	204	99	88	68
Arkansas River	11	1,473	1,510	940	880	15	87	225	127	165	161	128	255
		Percent distribution											
All areas	246	100.0	100.0	47.1	43.7	4.2	5.5	14.3	16.3	28.7	24.4	5.7	10.1
Atlantic Coast Plain	31	100.0	100.0	50.1	41.9	4.2	9.1	8.2	5.0	35.1	34.4	2.4	9.6
Black Belt (A)	31	100.0	100.0	46.4	41.5	7.5	6.6	26.2	21.5	13.5	23.3	6.4	7.1
Black Belt (B)	16	100.0	100.0	45.0	43.6	3.3	4.5	13.0	14.2	35.2	30.4	3.5	7.3
Upper Delta	79	100.0	100.0	52.1	48.8	1.0	5.3	9.9	12.6	32.9	25.6	4.1	7.7
Lower Delta	19	100.0	100.0	19.4	15.6	11.1	5.2	25.7	34.9	33.4	28.5	10.4	15.8
Interior Plain	17	100.0	100.0	51.5	50.6	7.4	2.1	14.3	20.0	24.2	20.3	2.6	7.0
Mississippi Bluffs	27	100.0	100.0	47.6	43.7	3.2	5.1	7.3	11.2	36.2	26.1	5.7	13.9
Red River	15	100.0	100.0	58.5	54.7	4.7	6.4	13.0	21.8	16.6	10.1	7.2	7.0
Arkansas River	11	100.0	100.0	63.8	58.2	1.0	5.8	15.3	8.4	11.2	10.7	8.7	16.9

[1] Farmsteads, roads, ditches, turnrows, streams, lakes, and low marshy areas not profitable to drain.

While the proportion of the total plantation acreage in pasture decreased by 2 percent between 1934 and 1937, a slight increase in woodland occurred. A relatively large acreage in woodland is important as wood is the chief type of fuel utilized by plantation families. A large proportion of the woodland on plantations is along streams, in hilly sections unsuited to cultivation, and in low wet areas which require drainage prior to cultivation.

The smallest proportion of the total plantation acreage except that devoted to idle cropland consists of (1) the area occupied by operator and tenant home sites, barns for livestock, space for implements, storehouses for farm products, gins, commissaries, and other plantation buildings; and (2) the area occupied by roads, ditches, turnrows, watercourses, lakes, and low marshy areas not likely to be profitable for cultivation even if drained. Between 1934 and 1937 the acreage included in these categories decreased significantly in all areas except the Red River Valley.

Thus, the general tendency in organization, as reflected in land use during the period covered, appears to be in the direction of more complete utilization of the plantation acreage. The average acreage devoted to crops and woodland increased, and, at the same time, idle cropland and the acreage devoted to farmsteads, roads, ditches, and wasteland were restricted.

Cotton Choppers With Riding Boss.

ORGANIZATION OF CROPLAND

Although the plantations studied were selected from cotton counties,[4] there was a wide range from area to area in the proportion of crop acres planted to cotton. All areas studied had from 30 to 60 percent of the crop acreage devoted to cotton during both years included in the study with the exception of the Black Belt (A) Area which dropped below 30 percent (appendix table 3). On individual plantations, however, the acreage occasionally dropped below 20 percent or rose to 80 percent or more (appendix table 4). A significant increase in the proportion of the total cropland planted to cotton occurred in 1937 when acreage reduction was on a voluntary basis as compared with 1934 when production restrictions were severe (table 5).

Table 5.—Organization of Cropland per Plantation,[1] 1937 and 1934 [2]

Crop	Crop acres per plantation			
	1937		1934	
	Number	Percent	Number	Percent
All crops	464	100.0	400	100.0
Cotton	230	49.6	178	44.5
Corn and interplanted legumes	134	28.0	148	37.0
Small grain [3]	18	3.9	13	3.3
Cowpea and soybean hay	20	4.3	14	3.5
Alfalfa hay	12	2.6	9	2.2
Other hay crops	9	1.9	9	2.2
Cowpeas and soybeans for seed	3	0.6	1	0.3
Truck, garden, and orchard	12	2.6	10	2.5
All other crops	26	5.6	18	4.5

[1] Excludes cropland of renters (cash and standing) for which data by crops were not available.
[2] For data by areas see appendix table 3.
[3] Principally oats.

Corn, like cotton, is planted on practically all plantations and ranks next to cotton in crop acreage. Practically all corn is interplanted with legumes, principally cowpeas, soybeans, and velvet beans. A slight reduction in corn acreage occurred between 1934 and 1937, probably because of the expansion in cropland devoted to cotton, hay crops, and crops planted for soil maintenance in compliance with the AAA soil conservation program. Cropland occupied by truck, gardens, and orchards increased slightly in the majority of the areas surveyed.

The remaining acreage was devoted for the most part to temporary pasture and soil maintenance. In the Atlantic Coast Plain and Black Belt (A) Areas, however, tobacco and peanuts occupied approximately 10 percent of the acreage in both years.

[4] Counties in which 40 percent or more of the gross farm income in 1930 was from cotton farms. Woofter, T. J., Jr. and Others, op. cit., p. 37.

Table 6.—Organization of Cropland per Plantation, by Tenure and Area, 1937 and 1934

Item	All areas		Atlantic Coast Plain		Black Belt (A)		Black Belt (B)		Upper Delta		Lower Delta		Interior Plain		Mississippi Bluffs		Red River		Arkansas River	
	1937	1934	1937	1934	1937	1934	1937	1934	1937	1934	1937	1934	1937	1934	1937	1934	1937	1934	1937	1934
Total plantations	246		31		31		16		79		19		17		27		15		11	
Crop acres per plantation	477	417	331	243	350	303	243	249	579	542	373	249	397	340	434	392	718	535	940	880
									Percent distribution											
Crop acres operated by:																				
Wage laborers [1]	40.7	35.6	37.9	38.6	34.5	38.9	25.8	36.9	40.8	34.6	10.8	23.3	49.9	24.0	36.1	21.2	62.3	60.0	52.7	42.6
Croppers	45.5	45.5	45.2	51.3	61.3	55.1	52.8	31.9	43.4	42.8	58.3	36.4	34.2	54.5	49.6	54.0	36.2	37.0	38.4	46.6
Share tenants	11.1	14.9	13.1	4.6	1.6	3.7	3.0	10.5	14.7	21.1	12.1	18.0	15.9	21.5	14.3	16.2	1.5	3.0	8.9	10.7
Renters (cash and standing) [2]	2.7	4.0	3.8	5.5	2.6	2.3	18.4	20.7	1.1	1.5	18.8	22.3	15.9	—	—	8.6	—	—	—	0.1
Wage laborer crop acres in:																				
Cotton	34.5	21.9	29.1	28.9	20.3	14.6	31.2	19.7	35.7	17.8	41.2	46.1	37.0	12.9	25.4	13.4	39.4	37.1	42.7	22.4
Corn	30.0	42.1	43.5	46.4	45.5	41.1	34.6	32.8	25.3	43.1	31.1	44.7	35.8	48.5	34.7	70.0	33.0	31.0	14.3	34.5
All other crops	35.5	36.0	27.4	24.7	34.2	44.3	34.2	47.5	39.0	39.1	27.7	9.2	27.2	38.6	39.9	16.6	27.6	31.9	43.0	43.1
Cropper crop acres in:																				
Cotton	60.1	59.1	34.0	31.6	34.4	34.5	39.5	45.2	73.0	62.8	45.8	54.3	55.1	56.1	63.8	59.5	85.3	79.1	68.0	90.2
Corn	27.2	32.0	36.9	40.3	42.8	49.0	37.8	48.2	22.8	30.0	19.3	37.6	42.5	40.1	31.9	31.7	10.2	20.2	12.0	9.1
All other crops	12.7	8.9	29.1	28.1	22.8	16.5	22.7	6.6	4.2	7.2	34.9	8.1	2.4	3.8	4.3	8.8	4.5	0.7	20.0	0.7
Share tenant crop acres in:																				
Cotton	59.4	54.3	26.4	22.6	37.4	44.7	45.7	46.3	65.4	55.9	61.2	46.9	49.4	43.8	54.0	56.9	98.2	57.6	82.5	71.4
Corn	31.6	37.0	38.5	37.1	50.3	49.0	38.8	36.3	29.3	43.4	28.7	46.4	41.0	34.7	40.5	4.1	—	29.7	15.6	28.2
All other crops	9.0	8.7	35.1	40.3	12.3	6.3	15.5	17.4	5.3	0.7	10.1	6.7	9.6	21.5	5.5	39.0	1.8	12.7	1.9	0.4

[1] Including nonresident laborers.
[2] Data by crops not available.

Organization of Cropland by Tenure

The relative importance of the various tenure groups [5] can be expressed in terms of the proportion of the total crop acreage operated by each type (table 6 and fig. 3). Croppers constituted the most important source of labor on the plantations studied, operating approximately 46 percent of all cropland during both years. Significant increases in acreage operated by croppers were noted in the Black

Fig. 3 – OPERATION OF CROP ACRES PER PLANTATION, BY TENURE
1937 and 1934

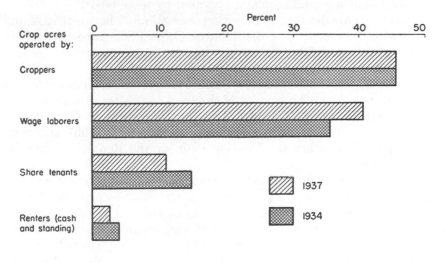

Source: Table 6   WPA 3306

---

[5] Definitions of tenure status were as follows:

Wage hand—An individual (with or without a family) who lives on the plantation and has a definite agreement with the operator to work for a more or less definite number of months at an agreed-upon wage.

Cropper—A family which has a definite agreement with the operator whereby the family furnishes only labor (operator furnishes work stock and implements) in cultivating an agreed-upon acreage and receives in return a specified share of the crop, usually one-half share or less.

Share tenant—A family which has a definite agreement with a landlord whereby the family furnishes some or all of the work stock and implements in cultivating an agreed-upon acreage and receives in return a share of the crop, usually more than one-half.

Cash renter—A family which pays cash for the use of the land.

Standing renter—A family which has a definite agreement with the landlord whereby the family pays a specified amount of crop produce (for example, 4 bales of cotton, 800 pounds of tobacco, etc.) and which operates independently of the landlord.

Belt (B) and Lower Delta Areas, but these increases were compensated for by decreases in a number of other areas.

Wage laborers constituted the second most important source of labor on the plantations studied. In 1937 an average of approximately 41 percent of the cropland was operated by this tenure group, an increase of 5 percent since 1934. During this period the proportion of the total cropland operated by wage laborers more than doubled in the Interior Plain Area while significant increases were also found in the Upper Delta, Mississippi Bluffs, and Arkansas River Areas. Most of the other areas had experienced a net loss since 1934 in the proportion of the total cropland operated by wage labor.

Share tenants declined in importance in all areas between 1934 and 1937 with the exception of the Atlantic Coast Plain Area where there was a net gain of about 9 percent in crop acreage operated by this type of labor.

Cash and standing renters, of little proportionate importance at best, operated a smaller percent of the total crop acreage in practically all areas in 1937 than in 1934. They had been completely ousted in the Mississippi Bluffs and Arkansas River Areas by 1937 and were not reported in either the Interior Plain or the Red River Area as early as 1934.

On the whole, the data show a tendency for wage laborers to increase in importance in the plantation areas of the Southeast at the expense of share tenants and renters. So far, in spite of important forces effecting changes in agricultural patterns, croppers have held their own on the plantations surveyed. This over-all picture, however, represents the results of major fluctuations from area to area, the most striking of which were pointed out above.

Related to the organization of cropland by tenure is the distribution of the crop acreage operated by each type of tenant. Approximately three-fifths of the cropland operated by croppers and share tenants was in cotton during both crop years (table 6 and fig. 4). The remainder of the acreage was principally in corn, while a relatively small acreage was planted to various hay and soil-conserving crops and to crops for human consumption. The proportion of the cropland operated by croppers and which was in cotton did not fluctuate greatly in most areas, but there was some tendency toward increases in the Upper Delta, Red River, Mississippi Bluffs, and Atlantic Coast Plain Areas and noticeable decreases in the Black Belt (B), Lower Delta, and Arkansas River Areas.

In the majority of the areas studied, the proportion of the cropland operated by share tenants which was in cotton increased. While the proportion in corn decreased, share tenants still had more crop acreage devoted to corn production than did croppers during both years. Thus, they provided at least part of the feed for their livestock.

Fig. 4 — ORGANIZATION OF CROPLAND PER PLANTATION, BY TENURE
1937 and 1934

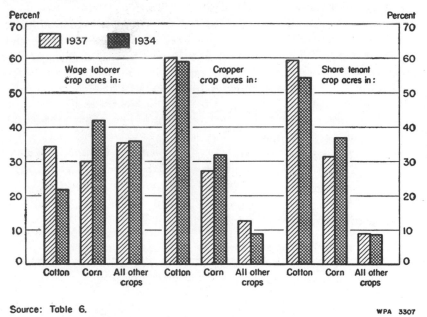

Source: Table 6.

WPA 3307

Not only did the proportion of all plantation crop acreage operated by wage laborers increase from 1934 to 1937 but also more of the cropland operated by wage laborers was in cotton for the crop year 1937 than 1934. The increase for all areas was from 22 percent of all cropland to 35 percent. Whereas the proportion of the acreage in cotton approximately doubled in the Upper Delta, Mississippi Bluffs, and Arkansas River Areas, it almost trebled in the Interior Plain Area. For all areas combined, additional crop acreage devoted to cotton in 1937 was at the expense of corn acreage, as the proportion of land in other crops cultivated by wage laborers remained practically the same. The upward trend in cotton acreage operated by wage laborers reflects the increase in large-scale production equipment. Under such conditions hand labor operations are performed largely by off-plantation labor and tenant occasional labor.

COTTON YIELD

The average yield of the major crop, cotton, increased from 268 pounds of lint cotton per acre in 1934 for all areas combined to 456 pounds in 1937 (appendix table 5). Factors influencing this marked rise in yield included more favorable climatic conditions, improved seed, increased use of commercial fertilizer, larger acreages planted to leguminous soil-building crops in 1936, inducements provided by the soil conservation program of the Agricultural Adjustment Administration, decreased damage from plant disease and insect infestation, and developments in methods of production.

For all areas the increased cotton yield was of approximately equal importance whether the land was operated by wage laborers, croppers, or share tenants. There were considerable variations in yield by area, however, which were probably influenced more by climatic conditions, soils, use of fertilizers, and timely cultivation than by the type of labor.

PLANTATION LIVESTOCK

Plantation livestock owned by the average operator increased from 1934 to 1937, although the numbers were still relatively small at the time of the later survey [6] (table 7). The fact that there was some increase in the various types of livestock in most areas is associated with the increased crop acreage and possibly with a tendency toward diversification and expanded production for home use.

Table 7.—Plantation Livestock,[1] by Area, 1937 and 1934

Area	Total planta-tions	Number per plantation							
		Mules and horses		Cows		Pigs		Chickens	
		1937	1934	1937	1934	1937	1934	1937	1934
All areas	246	20	16	28	16	31	16	51	56
Atlantic Coast Plain	31	11	9	7	3	34	14	73	52
Black Belt (A)	31	13	11	26	13	48	22	41	39
Black Belt (B)	16	9	8	7	9	13	7	69	68
Upper Delta	79	24	18	32	11	36	17	44	49
Lower Delta	19	13	10	57	45	32	13	39	92
Interior Plain	17	15	12	26	23	23	14	32	66
Mississippi Bluffs	27	21	18	22	13	24	9	69	61
Red River	15	38	30	37	53	16	20	22	68
Arkansas River	11	35	34	46	5	19	22	96	45

[1] Owned by the operator. No data were secured on the ownership of livestock by any type of tenants.

The average number of work stock per plantation, including both mules and horses, increased from 16 in 1934 to 20 in 1937. By areas, the increases ranged as high as one-third in the Upper Delta Area. The increase in cows per plantation from 16 to 28 was considerably more important than the increase in work stock. Significant increases in the average number of cows occurred in all areas except the Black Belt (B) and Red River Areas which experienced decreases. The numbers were increased 100 percent or more in the Atlantic Coast Plain, Black Belt (A), Upper Delta, and Arkansas River Areas.

The greatest livestock increase from 1934 to 1937 was in the number of pigs per plantation. For all areas combined the number practically

[6] No data were secured on the ownership of livestock by any type of tenants.

doubled.   Every area had a significant increase except the Red River and Arkansas River Areas where small reductions were made.

While the change in number of chickens per plantation from 1934 to 1937 for all areas was insignificant, the average number varied widely from area to area.   In all cases flocks were so small that they were obviously maintained only to supply the operators' households.

Hoe Work.

Chapter II

CHANGES IN PLANTATION LABOR AND POWER

THE PLANTATION operator's objective of managing his acreage efficiently in order to produce as large net returns as possible is directly related to the types and combinations of labor and power utilized.

LABOR

A major consideration affecting the plantation operator's organization and operation plans is the available labor supply. Since the plantations studied are principally devoted to cotton production, which requires large amounts of hand labor during chopping and picking seasons, the operator must consider the relative availability and economy of the various types of labor. Considerable changes in plantation labor organization may occur from year to year, reflecting changes in the total number of resident families and in the different types of labor utilized (appendix table 6).

The slight increase from 15 to 16 resident families per plantation in all areas from 1934 to 1937 (table 8 and fig. 5) can be attributed to

Table 8.—Resident Families [1] per Plantation, by Area and Type, 1937 and 1934

Area	Total planta-tions	Resident families per plantation									
		Total		Wage laborer		Cropper		Share tenant		Renter (cash and standing)	
		1937	1934	1937	1934	1937	1934	1937	1934	1937	1934
All areas	246	16.3	15.2	2.5	2.2	10.5	9.7	2.9	2.7	0.4	0.6
Atlantic Coast Plain	31	8.7	7.7	3.1	2.6	4.1	4.4	1.2	0.3	0.3	0.4
Black Belt (A)	31	8.5	7.7	2.8	2.3	5.1	4.7	0.3	0.5	0.3	0.2
Black Belt (B)	16	6.8	7.1	1.9	2.1	3.9	3.1	0.3	0.8	0.7	1.1
Upper Delta	79	23.1	20.1	2.7	1.6	14.1	13.1	6.2	5.2	0.1	0.2
Lower Delta	19	16.5	14.0	0.2	0.7	10.9	6.4	2.2	3.3	3.2	3.6
Interior Plain	17	10.6	9.8	4.2	2.2	4.8	6.0	1.6	1.6	—	—
Mississippi Bluffs	27	15.0	16.7	0.7	1.4	11.9	11.0	2.4	2.9	—	1.4
Red River	15	20.3	18.3	4.7	4.5	15.3	13.2	0.3	0.6	—	—
Arkansas River	11	31.6	36.3	2.4	6.1	26.7	26.6	2.5	3.5	—	0.1

[1] Excludes displaced families.

increases in cropland operated, especially in the proportion of cropland planted to cotton. This resulted in increased requirements for hand labor to cultivate and harvest the expanded acreage. Wide variations among areas in the number of resident families per plantation reflect differences in the size of plantation operations. The only areas having fewer families per plantation in 1937 than in 1934 were the Black Belt (B), Mississippi Bluffs, and Arkansas River Areas.

Fig. 5 – RESIDENT FAMILIES PER PLANTATION, BY TYPE
1937 and 1934

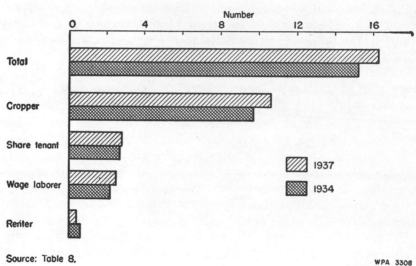

Source: Table 8.

WPA 3308

Croppers were the most important type of plantation labor during both periods and accounted for approximately two-thirds of all resident families. There was a slight increase from 1934 to 1937 in the average number of cropper families per plantation and in the number of plantations operated by croppers only (table 8 and appendix table 7).

In order adequately to measure changes in labor, since both crop acreage and resident families per plantation increased between 1934 and 1937, it was necessary to hold the acreage factor constant. This was accomplished by computing the number of resident families per 1,000 acres of cropland (appendix table 8). The average number of such families declined from almost 37 in 1934 to 34 in 1937. All areas reported a decrease in the number of resident families per 1,000 acres of cropland except the Upper Delta Area which had an increase of about 8 percent. The Atlantic Coast Plain, Lower Delta, Mississippi Bluffs, Red River, and Arkansas River Areas showed the most significant decreases.

While the total number of resident families per 1,000 acres of cropland declined only slightly from 1934 to 1937, the tenure status of these families changed considerably. Renters (cash and standing) had the greatest proportionate decline with only one-half as many families of this type per 1,000 acres of cropland in 1937 as in 1934 (appendix table 8). Slight declines occurred in the share tenant and cropper groups, whereas wage laborer families held their own.

Predominance of Negro Labor

Traditionally the Negro resident family has been the major source of labor for plantations. The plantations surveyed reported approximately nine Negro families for every white family in both 1937 and 1934.[1] The majority of the plantations were operated entirely by Negro tenants, and a slight increase in the proportion with only Negro families had occurred between 1934 and 1937 (table 9). Moreover, only a small number of plantations were operated entirely by white tenants, while approximately 37 percent of the plantations in 1937 as compared with 40 percent in 1934 were operated by both white and Negro tenants.

Table 9.—Color of Tenants on Plantations, by Area, 1937 and 1934

Area	Total	Number of plantations, by color of tenants					
		White		Negro		Both	
		1937	1934	1937	1934	1937	1934
All areas:							
Number	246	5	3	150	145	91	98
Percent	100.0	2.0	1.2	61.0	59.0	37.0	39.8
Atlantic Coast Plain	31	—	—	13	15	18	16
Black Belt (A)	31	2	1	17	16	12	14
Black Belt (B)	16	—	—	8	8	8	8
Upper Delta	79	3	2	52	53	24	24
Lower Delta	19	—	—	12	15	7	4
Interior Plain	17	—	—	10	8	7	9
Mississippi Bluffs	27	—	—	22	17	5	10
Red River	15	—	—	7	8	8	7
Arkansas River	11	—	—	9	5	2	6

Utilization of Off-Plantation Labor

The expansion in cotton acreage and the high yields in the good cotton year 1937 increased the demand for off-plantation seasonal labor. Approximately 53 percent of the plantations studied reported using some off-plantation seasonal labor for cotton chopping and picking, although the proportions varied widely among areas (table 10). In the Red River Area more than four out of five of the planta-

---

[1] Data on file in the Division of Research, Work Projects Administration. Washington, D. C.

tions used off-plantation seasonal labor, while in the Black Belt (A), Upper Delta, and Mississippi Bluffs Areas about two out of three plantations used this type of labor.

Table 10.—Cotton Acreage Chopped or Picked by Off-Plantation Labor, by Area and Tenure of Operator, 1937

Area	Plantations reporting off-plantation labor	Percent[1] of cotton acreage chopped by off-plantation labor			Percent[1] of cotton acreage picked by off-plantation labor		
		Owner-operator[2]	Cropper	Share tenant	Owner-operator[2]	Cropper	Share tenant
All areas	130	17	1	5	36	11	12
Atlantic Coast Plain	12	12	—	19	32	1	19
Black Belt (A)	19	18	1	3	36	9	17
Black Belt (B)	4	—	3	—	5	3	—
Upper Delta	54	20	2	8	42	11	14
Lower Delta	5	28	4	—	28	12	—
Interior Plain	2	11	2	—	9	8	15
Mississippi Bluffs	16	11	1	—	39	16	16
Red River	13	9	—	—	41	13	10
Arkansas River	5	29	2	—	34	14	—

[1] Weighted average.
[2] Cultivated by wage labor.

Although less than one-fifth [2] of the total cotton acreage of the owner-operators in all areas was chopped by off-plantation seasonal labor, the proportion rose to more than one-fourth in the Lower Delta and Arkansas River Areas. The percent of the total cotton acreage of croppers and share tenants chopped by off-plantation seasonal labor was insignificant except for share tenants in the Atlantic Coast Plain Area.

The increase in cotton acreage plus a high yield per acre also required additional labor for picking the 1937 crop. More than one-third of the owner-operators' cotton was picked by off-plantation seasonal labor. Only the operators in the Black Belt (B) and Interior Plain Areas made little use of off-plantation labor for picking. Although the proportions of the cropper and share tenant cotton picked by off-plantation seasonal labor were only 11 and 12 percent, respectively, for all areas, it is significant that the volume of production exceeded the amount the family labor supply could pick.

Type of Off-Plantation Labor

Nonresident seasonal labor was of two types: (1) laborers living within daily commuting distance of the plantation who were classified as local laborers, and (2) laborers who remained on the plantation premises during the period of seasonal employment. This latter group was composed of migratory laborers.

[2] Weighted average.

One-half Row Cotton Cultivation.

Transportation

During the cotton-chopping period of the 1937 crop season, the majority of the local seasonal laborers furnished their own transportation, although the operators of 15 plantations reported transporting laborers, mostly from neighboring towns and villages (appendix table 9). The average distance traveled to work by local laborers employed for cotton chopping was 2 miles. On the other hand, plantation operators using migratory labor had to furnish all of the transportation, and the laborers came an average distance of 15 miles.

During the cotton-picking season a much larger number of plantations used nonresident seasonal labor. Local laborers, who were employed on 89 plantations, again usually furnished their own transportation, although the average distance traveled by this type of labor was extended to 4 miles. The operators of 35 plantations provided the transportation for their local off-plantation labor. Moreover, 30 of the 34 operators using migratory laborers for cotton picking furnished the transportation. These laborers were usually brought in by truck. The average distance between the place migratory laborers were recruited and the plantation on which they were employed was 79 miles.

CHANGES IN POWER

An increase in the average number of work stock per plantation between 1934 and 1937 was reported for all areas as a result of the significant increase in crop acreage (table 11). In most areas, however, the number of work stock per 1,000 acres of cropland remained about stationary. The Upper Delta was the only area in which an

Table 11.—Power per Plantation and per 1,000 Acres of Cropland, by Area, 1937 and 1934

Area	Total plantations	Crop acres per plantation [1]		Work stock				Tractors			
				Per plantation		Per 1,000 acres of cropland		Per plantation		Per 1,000 acres of cropland	
		1937	1934	1937	1934	1937	1934	1937	1934	1937	1934
All areas	246	411	338	20	16	49	47	0.9	0.6	2.2	1.8
Atlantic Coast Plain	31	275	219	11	9	40	41	0.4	0.3	1.5	1.4
Black Belt (A)	31	335	285	13	11	39	39	0.3	0.2	0.9	0.7
Black Belt (B)	16	191	171	9	8	47	47	0.6	0.1	3.1	0.6
Upper Delta	79	487	419	24	18	49	43	1.6	1.1	3.3	2.6
Lower Delta	19	258	149	13	10	50	67	0.7	0.5	2.7	3.4
Interior Plain	17	334	267	15	12	45	45	0.1	0.1	0.3	0.4
Mississippi Bluffs	27	372	295	21	18	56	61	0.8	0.3	2.2	1.0
Red River	15	707	519	38	30	54	58	1.9	1.0	2.7	1.9
Arkansas River	11	856	784	35	34	41	43	1.5	1.4	1.8	1.8

[1] Operated by wage laborers and croppers only. Acreage of share tenants and renters was operated with tenant-owned power.

important expansion in the use of work stock in relation to crop acreage was reported.

Animal power was supplemented in 1937 by an average of 0.9 tractors per plantation, an increase of 50 percent since 1934. Increases in the number of tractors per plantation were reported in all areas except the Interior Plain.

Because of the wide variation in the number and ultilization of tractors in the areas studied, the relative importance of the tractor as a source of plantation power cannot be definitely determined, but its increasing significance is obvious.[3] While the number of work stock per 1,000 acres of cropland increased from 47 to 49 for all areas combined between 1934 and 1937, tractors increased from 1.8 to 2.2 per 1,000 acres. Moreover, the increase in work stock per 1,000 acres of cropland was confined to the Upper Delta Area while tractor power increased on this basis in all areas except the Lower Delta, Interior Plain, and Arkansas River Areas.

The wide variation in the number of work stock and tractors per 1,000 acres of cropland was largely due to the utilization of both types of power on the same plantations. In 1937 more than one-half of the plantations surveyed used combinations of work stock and tractors for power (table 12). During this crop year only 2 plantations used tractor power exclusively, while 113 plantations still depended entirely on work stock. Of the 133 plantations reporting tractors in 1937, 64 reported 1 tractor, 47 reported 2 tractors, and 22 reported 3 or more tractors (table 13 and fig. 6).

Table 12.—Type of Power Used on Plantations, by Area, 1937

Area	Total plantations	Type of power		
		Work stock only	Tractor only	Work stock and tractor
All areas	246	113	2	131
Atlantic Coast Plain	31	20	—	11
Black Belt (A)	31	23	—	8
Black Belt (B)	16	12	—	4
Upper Delta	79	15	1	63
Lower Delta	19	10	—	9
Interior Plain	17	15	—	2
Mississippi Bluffs	27	13	—	14
Red River	15	2	1	12
Arkansas River	11	3	—	8

[3] "Although the greatest degree of mechanization is found in the North Central States, the highest rates of recent mechanization are found in the South and Southwest. Mississippi leads the Old South both in number of tractors added since 1930 and in the rate of increase; the number of tractors increasing from 5,542 in 1930 to 14,703 in 1938, an increase of 165 percent." Hamilton, C. Horace, "The Social Effects of Recent Trends in the Mechanization of Agriculture," *Rural Sociology*, Vol. 4, 1939, pp. 6–7.

One-Row Cotton Cultivation.

Table 13.—Number of Tractors per Plantation, by Area, 1937

Area	Total plantations reporting tractors	Number of tractors		
		1	2	3 or more
All areas	133	64	47	22
Atlantic Coast Plain	11	9	2	—
Black Belt (A)	8	6	2	—
Black Belt (B)	4	3	1	—
Upper Delta	64	29	21	14
Lower Delta	9	4	5	—
Interior Plain	2	—	2	—
Mississippi Bluffs	14	5	6	3
Red River	13	5	5	3
Arkansas River	8	3	3	2

Fig. 6 – TRACTORS PER PLANTATION, 1937

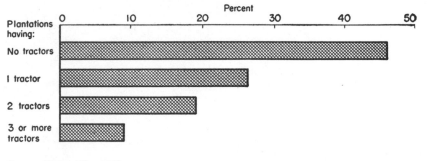

Source: Tables 12 and 13.   WPA 3309

The crop acreage handled by tractor and work stock combinations in the various operations involved in cotton production indicates the importance of tractors on plantations (appendix table 10). Almost two-fifths of the crop acreage flatbroken in 1937 was handled by tractors. In the Mississippi Bluffs and Red River Areas tractors were used for more than 50 percent of the flatbreaking. In other areas the practice was followed for 7 to 47 percent of the acreage. In seedbed preparation, i. e., preparation of land for planting, approximately one-third of the total crop acreage was handled by tractors, whereas among individual areas the use of tractors ranged from 2 percent of the acreage in the Black Belt (B) Area to 57 percent in the Red River Area. In planting, work stock were used on four-fifths of the acreage in 1937. As a matter of fact, 57 percent of the planting in all areas was done with one-horse equipment. The preference for the use of work stock for cultivating as well as planting is shown by the fact that only one-fifth of the crop acreage was cultivated with tractors.

The increasing use of mechanized power has several important corollaries. For one thing it will decrease the need for feed production for livestock and, with unrestricted cotton production, might induce operators to plant an even higher proportion of cropland to cotton than in the past. Another change associated with the increase in mechanization has been the trend toward an increase in the proportion of total cropland and of cotton acreage operated with wage labor.[4]

Plantation operators were asked to give, in order of their importance, factors which, in their opinion, were retarding the shift toward greater mechanization. The major factor as reported by the operators was the lack of available capital at a low rate of interest (table 14). Labor was given as the second major factor hindering the shift to mechanized power. This was due to the need for an adequate labor supply during the peak seasons of chopping and picking cotton and to the lack of skilled tractor operators.

Table 14.—Factors Retarding Mechanization as Reported by Operators, 1937

Factors retarding mechanization	Operators reporting [1]
Problem of financing purchase	119
Labor	98
Unsuitable land	74
Lesser efficiency of tractors	21
Preference for work stock	19
Sufficient supply of work stock	15
Size of plantation	14
Other	22

[1] In some cases operators reported more than 1 factor.

A number of operators reported that the size of their plantations and the prevalence of small irregular-shaped fields retarded their shift to greater mechanization. Tractors were definitely specified as less efficient than work stock, especially for the cultivation of crops, by 21 operators, while 34 operators preferred using work stock or had an ample number for plantation operation.

Mechanization has not been the only factor responsible for the reduction in the number of resident families per 1,000 acres of cropland, but tractors have played a major role in this reduction. In 1934 there were about 25 resident families per tractor on the plantations surveyed, but by 1937 there were only 18 resident families per tractor [5] as a result of increased mechanization.

PROSPECTS FOR INCREASED MECHANIZATION

Within the areas studied rather large acreages of level cropland are subject to mechanization. The fact that mechanization or even

[4] See also Langsford, E. L. and Thibodeaux, B. H., *Plantation Organization and Operation in the Yazoo-Mississippi Delta Area*, Technical Bulletin No. 682, U. S. Department of Agriculture, Washington, D. C., May 1939, pp. 27 and 54.

[5] Data on file in the Division of Research, Work Projects Administration, Washington, D. C.

larger horse-drawn equipment is less economical on small irregular-shaped fields, very sandy soils, and a hilly topography than one- or two-horse equipment, however, together with the availability of large amounts of family labor which have little or no alternative employment, will continue to be important retarding factors in the increased mechanization in the Southeast.

Cotton, more than any other major crop, has resisted the general trend toward mechanization in agriculture, and such mechanization as has taken place to date has involved only part of the major operations in cultivation. Thinning and hoeing, like picking, are tasks that still require an immense amount of tedious hand labor.

A considerable saving in labor in cotton production prior to harvest might be effected through the use of one-row equipment instead of the one-half row equipment now being used in seedbed preparation and cultivation on a large number of plantations. Furthermore, a considerable proportion of the labor of hoeing and chopping might be eliminated by the use of a hill-dropper planter and delinted seed. Mechanical means of performing the chopping operation have been devised but as yet they are in the early stages of development. The mechanical cotton chopper, even if perfected, together with complete mechanization of seedbed preparation, planting, and cultivating will not remove completely the need for hoe labor, especially in areas of heavy rainfall, which is conducive to heavy weed growth.

Although an increase in the number of plantations using various laborsaving devices for preharvest operations may be expected, the rate of adoption in the areas surveyed will be gradual and will even be retarded by the fact that large amounts of labor are needed for picking. In many cases it will continue to be economically advantageous to insure an adequate supply of harvest labor by employing the laborers throughout the year.

The perfection of an efficient and economical mechanical cotton picker would serve to a large extent to remove harvesting operations as an obstacle in areas suitable for mechanization. The use of such a machine would no doubt provide an important stimulus toward the use of large-scale equipment for preharvest operations as well and would thus result in the displacement of many agricultural workers. There seems little cause for alarm at the present time, however, even though certain cotton-picking machines are reported to have approached practical usefulness. Any adoption of such machinery may be expected to be very gradual as long as cheap labor is readily available.[6]

[6] Horne, Roman L. and McKibben, Eugene G., *Changes in Farm Power and Equipment: Mechanical Cotton Picker*, Report No. A–2, National Research Project, Works Progress Administration, Philadelphia, Pa., August 1937, p. 18.

Problems which still remain to be solved are the production of mechanically harvested, high-grade cotton; the overcoming of the difficulties in ginning mechanically picked cotton; and the breeding of new strains of cotton varieties that will make for better "pickability" on the part of mechanical pickers.[7]   Taking into account all of the factors in the situation, therefore, one is forced to agree with E. A. Johnston of the International Harvester Company "that there is absolutely no likelihood of mechanical cotton harvesters being produced and sold in quantities sufficient to revolutionize agriculture in the cotton-growing areas in the near future." [8]

[7] Bennett, Charles A., "The Relation of Mechanical Harvesting to the Production of High-Grade Cotton," *Agricultural Engineering*, Vol. 19, September 1938, p. 388.

[8] "The Evolution of the Mechanical Cotton Harvester," *Agricultural Engineering*, Vol. 19, September 1938, p. 388.

Four-Row Cotton Cultivation.

Chapter III

CREDIT

A PLANTATION is a business enterprise for which the operator may use credit to provide capital assets and to meet current operating expenses. Loans obtained for investment in fixed assets are secured by mortgages on the plantation and are classified as long-term debts. Loans for current operating expenses are short-term loans and are usually secured by chattel mortgages on the crop, livestock, and equipment.

OPERATORS' LONG-TERM INDEBTEDNESS

As a result of increased plantation profits operators have been enabled to liquidate part of their debts in recent years. The number reporting long-term indebtedness declined by 22 percent between 1934 and 1937, and at the same time the operators with debts reduced their indebtedness from an average of $13,018 to $11,914 or about 8 percent (table 15). Wide differences appeared among areas, although the number reporting long-term debts decreased in all areas except the Black Belt (A) and Lower Delta Areas (appendix table 11). During the same period the indebtedness per operator reporting was materially reduced in all areas except the Black Belt (B), Upper Delta, and Mississippi Bluffs Areas.

Among long-term loans, mortgages and bank and merchant loans had decreased in relative importance since 1934, while loans from governmental credit agencies, by open accounts, and from other sources rose correspondingly. The increases can be attributed not only to expanded credit facilities and to lower interest rates by governmental rather than other agencies but also to the fact that, as the plantation operators were able to repay their obligations, further credit channels were opened up.

Mortgages were the predominant type of long-term debt in both years. There was a definite trend toward an increase in Government

23

loans as a result of refinancing at a lower rate of interest (appendix table 12). Mortgages of all types showed lower annual rates of interest in 1937 than in 1934; the average rate declined from 5.6 percent to 4.8 percent.

Table 15.—Operators' Long-Term Debts, by Type, 1937 and 1934 [1]

Item	1937	1934
Total operators	246	246
Operators reporting debts	100	128
Debt per operator reporting debts	$11,914	$13,018
Percent of operators with debts reporting specified type of debt: [2]		
Mortgage	82.0	89.1
Bank	8.0	10.2
Merchant	1.0	1.6
Open account	2.0	0.8
Government	9.0	3.1
Other	4.0	2.3

[1] For data by areas see appendix table 11.
[2] Some operators reported more than 1 type of debt.

OPERATORS' SHORT-TERM CREDIT

Since the plantation operator is usually the primary source of credit for tenant families (except renters), he must be able to secure adequate credit facilities not only for plantation crop production but also for subsistence advances to resident families.[1] In many cases the operator secures production credit from several sources and reallocates part of this credit to his tenant families at an increased rate of interest. Security for short-term credit is generally a first lien on crops under cultivation, especially the major money crop which in this case is cotton. When a first lien is held by the lending agency on this crop, other liens may be made against livestock and implements. Thus, while credit agencies look to the plantation operator directly for repayment, the operator looks to his tenants both for his share of net profits and for repayment of his credit advances.

Banks were the principal source of short-term loans in both 1937 and 1934 although there was a marked reduction between the two years in the proportion of operators using this type of credit (table 16). Credit secured from merchants also decreased in importance as an increasing number of operators obtained credit from governmental agencies. Fertilizer companies, while the least important source of credit in each year, provided credit for twice as many operators in 1937 as in 1934. The number of operators obtaining loans was somewhat less than the total number of loans reported as some operators reported borrowing from more than one source.

[1] See pp. 26–28.

The average amounts of credit obtained from Government agencies and fertilizer companies had more than doubled since 1934, while loans secured from banks had increased by about one-third (table 16). On the other hand, merchant credit for 1937 operations was less than one-half of the 1934 average amount. The duration of these loans was usually 3 to 4 months regardless of the source.

Table 16.—Operators' Short-Term Credit, by Type,[1] Amount, and Duration of Loan and Annual Rate of Interest, 1937 and 1934 [2]

Type of loan	Operators reporting short-term credit		Average [3]					
			Amount of loan		Duration in months		Annual rate of interest	
	1937	1934	1937	1934	1937	1934	1937	1934
Government	38	30	$5,095	$2,326	3.5	3.1	11.9	11.8
Merchant	9	13	1,275	2,919	3.4	3.9	16.6	16.0
Fertilizer	6	3	893	300	2.8	3.7	22.9	30.0
Bank	65	109	3,098	2,349	3.3	3.4	16.0	15.3

[1] A small number of plantations reported current loans of other than the specified types. Also, 2 plantations reported Government loans and 1 plantation a bank loan in 1937 and 2 plantations merchant loans and 4 plantations bank loans in 1934, but did not give the amount of the loans or of the interest.
[2] For data by areas see appendix table 13.
[3] Arithmetic mean.

Usury laws are inoperative under the one-crop cotton plantation system insofar as legal rates of interest are involved. Practically all short-term credit is based on a per annum rate regardless of the length of time for which the advance is made. Although plantation operators and tenants alike use credit for periods usually from 3 to 8 months, they pay interest for a full year. Thus, an operator or tenant using $100 at 10 percent for 4 months must pay $10, a rate of 30 percent per annum.

Slight increases occurred in the annual rate of interest for Government, merchant, and bank loans between 1934 and 1937, but the average annual interest rate for the relatively unimportant fertilizer loans declined from 30 percent to 23 percent. Although interest on Government loans was lower than on other types, it too was extremely high, averaging almost 12 percent per annum in both years.

By areas, the number of operators reporting the various types of loans was usually too small to provide a basis for comparison (appendix table 13). Interest rates were consistently high from area to area but the Atlantic Coast Plain and Black Belt (A) Areas had particularly exorbitant annual rates of interest for merchant and fertilizer loans.

Although the total number of families on the plantations whose operators reported borrowing for current expenses declined by approximately 40 percent, the average amount borrowed per plantation and per family rose (table 17). The increases were 44 percent and 57 percent, respectively. In 1937 borrowing for production averaged $3,532 per plantation and $252 per resident family. With few exceptions, marked increases in borrowing per plantation and per family were reported for plantations with widely varying numbers of resident families.

Table 17.—Operators' Short-Term Credit, by Number of Resident Families, 1937 and 1934

Number of resident families	Operators reporting credit		Total families		Amount of credit			
					Per plantation		Per family	
	1937	1934	1937	1934	1937	1934	1937	1934
Total	101	157	1,415	2,388	$3,532	$2,455	$252	$161
Fewer than 10 families	53	75	269	482	1,796	1,029	354	160
10–14 families	21	26	258	304	3,339	2,090	272	179
15–19 families	4	16	64	273	4,800	3,276	300	192
20–24 families	6	15	136	324	6,325	2,853	279	132
25–29 families	6	8	163	217	6,550	3,813	241	141
30–34 families	1	6	33	195	6,000	6,083	182	187
35–39 families	—	2	—	74	—	6,975	—	189
40 families or more	10	9	492	519	8,898	8,633	181	150

TENANTS' SHORT-TERM CREDIT

The availability of short-term credit is related to tenure. The renter may secure credit from the plantation operator or negotiate loans elsewhere, offering liens on his cash crop, livestock, and implements as security. In contrast, the cropper is dependent upon the plantation operator for credit, both for current crop expenses and for subsistence, and can offer only a lien on his crop as security. In addition to his crop the share tenant can offer as security such farming equipment as he may own, but he too must generally rely on the plantation operator and not on outside sources for credit.

Tenants are usually advanced all of their share of current crop expenses prior to the beginning of the cotton harvest. In addition, subsistence or living expenses are advanced during the crop-cultivating season, extending ordinarily from the beginning of March to the latter part of August or into September. In years following disastrously low incomes, however, credit advances for tenant living may begin as early as January,[2] and some plantation operators make advances to their tenants throughout the year. The tenant's share of the value of cottonseed above ginning charges usually is sufficient to provide for his living expenses during the cotton harvest period, and his returns after settling with the landlord for the crop carry him through the winter months.

[2] Langsford, E. L. and Thibodeaux, B. H., *Plantation Organization and Operation in the Yazoo-Mississippi Delta Area*, Technical Bulletin No. 682, U. S. Department of Agriculture, Washington, D. C., May 1939, p. 47.

Collecting Cotton Pickers.

The total amount of credit advanced by the plantation operator per tenant family is determined largely by the prospective value of the current cotton crop. It is also influenced by the individual tenant's gain or loss during the preceding year. Upon the basis of these factors the plantation operator decides upon the amount of credit he can safely advance.

The dependence of tenants upon plantation operators for subsistence advances is shown by the fact that approximately 9 out of 10 plantations made such advances in both 1937 and 1934 (table 18). Although there had been a slight decline since 1934 in the number of plantations advancing subsistence, the amount advanced per family per month was larger in 1937 in all areas except the Black Belt (B), Interior Plain, and Red River Areas. For all areas combined the average monthly advance rose from $13.70 to $14.50. This suggests a slightly better economic situation among plantation families. Because of increased prices for the items the plantation family must buy, however, it is doubtful if any real improvement in living conditions occurred. Regardless of whether there was any advance, it is obvious that such limited amounts, coupled with the general inadequacy of production for home use, could provide only for an extremely low level of living.

The number of months during which subsistence was advanced did not change significantly on the average. A substantially shorter period was reported for the Atlantic Coast Plain, Interior Plain, and Red River Areas, however, and a longer period for the Black Belt (B) Area.

Under the short-term plantation credit system whereby the plantation operator is the guarantor to the lending agencies, he assumes the risk of crop success or failure. In order to lower his risk the operator raises the tenant's rate of interest above the rate he himself pays to allow for crop losses and for defaults, good risks among tenants tending to compensate for poor risks. Since fertilizer and seed loans are made to the tenant at the beginning of the crop season, the interest paid is for a loan carried throughout the season. In contrast the tenant is advanced a specified sum each month for subsistence. Such advances may begin in April and repayment be made in October, but the tenant pays interest on the total monthly advances for 6 months although he uses only one-sixth of the total amount for 6 months and one-sixth for as short a period as 1 month.

The average duration of subsistence advances to tenants on all plantations studied decreased slightly from 3.6 months in 1934 to 3.4 months in 1937 (appendix table 14). At the same time, the weighted annual rate of interest declined from about 40 percent to 36 percent. Even so, the rates remained two to three times as high as those paid by operators for short-term credit. Significant decreases in tenant interest rates on subsistence advances occurred in the Black Belt (B) and Arkansas River Areas. All other areas showed slight reductions in average annual interest rates except the Interior Plain and Red River Areas.

Table 18.—Practice of Operators in Granting Subsistence Advances, by Area, 1937 and 1934

Area	Total operators	Operators reporting amount of advances	Advance per family per month	Operators reporting number of months families received advances	Months families received advances							Average[1] number of months families received advances
					Less than 5	5	6	7	8	9 or 10	11 or 12	
All areas:												
1937	246	[2]208	$14.50	215	4	46	88	21	24	8	24	6.9
1934	246	[3]224	13.70	224	10	17	94	19	40	33	11	7.1
Atlantic Coast Plain:												
1937	31	24	15.10	24	1	2	3	2	7	3	6	8.4
1934	31	27	12.20	27	—	—	2	2	7	12	4	9.2
Black Belt (A):												
1937	31	25	12.20	25	—	2	4	10	4	1	4	7.8
1934	31	28	11.30	28	1	—	8	4	7	6	2	7.7
Black Belt (B):												
1937	16	16	11.50	16	—	1	5	2	2	1	5	8.4
1934	16	16	11.50	16	—	—	7	1	7	1	—	7.2
Upper Delta:												
1937	79	71	16.20	71	1	14	38	4	9	—	5	6.5
1934	79	73	15.60	73	3	4	46	5	4	10	1	6.7
Lower Delta:												
1937	19	8	11.30	15	1	1	10	—	—	2	1	6.7
1934	19	15	8.90	15	3	2	3	—	4	3	—	6.6
Interior Plain:												
1937	17	15	13.10	15	—	10	3	1	—	—	1	5.8
1934	17	17	18.10	17	—	2	6	1	7	—	1	7.1
Mississippi Bluffs:												
1937	27	27	14.70	27	—	5	20	—	1	—	1	6.1
1934	27	27	12.40	27	2	3	17	3	1	1	—	6.1
Red River:												
1937	15	12	13.60	12	—	6	3	2	—	1	—	6.0
1934	15	10	17.60	10	—	2	3	1	2	—	2	7.5
Arkansas River:												
1937	11	10	17.70	10	1	5	2	—	1	—	1	6.0
1934	11	11	14.30	11	1	4	2	2	1	—	1	6.3

[1] Arithmetic mean.
[2] Data not available for 1 plantation in the Upper Delta Area, and data for 7 plantations in the Lower Delta Area included interest on advances. With these 7 included, the average for the Lower Delta Area would have been $12.30.
[3] Data not available for 1 plantation in the Black Belt (A) Area.

The high interest rates paid by tenants are a major factor in preventing their rise up the agricultural ladder. The interest rates increase indebtedness to such an extent that they automatically bar any accumulation of resources by a large proportion of all plantation families. At the same time, pressure to pay off debts through production and sale of a cash crop is a strong influence against diversification and the production of varied field and garden crops for home consumption.

Chapter IV

PLANTATION INCOME

THE FINANCIAL operations involved in plantation management are complicated by the variety of activities engaged in. These normally expand as the size of the unit and number of resident families increase. The total investment varies widely among individual units but generally represents a rather heavy capital outlay. The long-term debts of many plantations are due to this outlay. Furthermore, current plantation operating expenses are usually large because the operator must furnish working capital for himself and his tenants. When crops are harvested, the operator generally assumes the marketing responsibility in order to guarantee the repayment of the principal and interest on credit advanced to tenants. In many cases pressure is exerted by the lending agencies for repayment of the operator's debts, thus making immediate sale of the product necessary even though it involves lower prices for the plantation operator. The expansion of the plantation unit, especially an increase in crop acreage, changes in the proportions of cropland planted to cotton and other crops, variations in yield, changes in both type and amount of labor, expansion of mechanization, differences in payments received for participation in the Agricultural Adjustment Administration program, and variations in the ratio of prices paid to those received for plantation commodities (appendix table 15) have definite effects on current expenditures and on gross and net plantation incomes.

INVESTMENT PER PLANTATION

To obtain plantation investment, field enumerators were instructed to enter values for land, buildings, livestock, and machinery at conservative market values, not at low assessed or high speculative values. The value of gins, commissaries, and the operator's residence if off the plantation was omitted.

The investment per plantation for all areas increased from $31,378 in 1934 to $37,504 in 1937 or by about one-fifth (table 19). Moreover, all areas reported significant increases except the Black Belt (B), Interior Plain, and Red River Areas which had had definite decreases in investment per plantation since 1934 (appendix table 16).

Table 19.—Investment per Plantation [1] and per Crop Acre for Land, Buildings, Livestock, and Machinery, 1937 and 1934 [2]

Item	Investment per plantation				Investment per crop acre	
	1937		1934		1937	1934
	Amount	Percent	Amount	Percent		
Total	$37,504	100.0	$31,378	100.0	$79	$75
Land	27,874	74.3	23,484	74.8	58	56
Buildings	4,814	12.8	4,366	13.9	10	10
Livestock	2,947	7.9	1,996	6.4	6	5
Machinery	1,869	5.0	1,532	4.9	5	4

[1] Data not available for 1 plantation in the Lower Delta Area in 1937 and for 2 plantations in the Black Belt (B) Area, 1 plantation in the Upper Delta Area, and 2 plantations in the Arkansas River Area in 1934.
[2] For data by areas see appendix table 16.

Among the plantations surveyed, slightly less than 75 percent of the total average investment was in land. The proportionate investment in buildings declined slightly from 1934 to 1937, as expansion in buildings failed to keep pace with expansion in acreage. Investments in livestock and in machinery both showed tendencies to increase and constituted approximately 8 and 5 percent, respectively, of the total in 1937. There was considerable variation among areas in the proportion of the total investment allocated to land, buildings, livestock, and machinery (appendix table 16). Land, for example, accounted for from less than two-thirds to more than four-fifths of the total in the various areas.

For all plantations investment per crop acre rose from $75 in 1934 to $79 in 1937, although only four of the nine areas had increases. The investment in land, livestock, and machinery per crop acre increased, while the investment in buildings remained the same.

GROSS PLANTATION INCOME

As obtained in the survey, gross income per plantation included current cash receipts from farming operations only for the crop years 1937 and 1934, respectively. Financial returns from plantation-operated nonfarm enterprises, such as commissaries and cotton gins, and inventories of plantation-owned seed and feed on hand were not reported. Furthermore, no attempt was made to evaluate commodities produced for home consumption nor to place values on perquisites, such as house rent, wood, and water, which were free to families living on the plantations. Cash benefits received from participation in the AAA program were credited to the crop year to which they applied even if payment was received in subsequent years. Likewise, farm products held for speculation were considered for the purposes of this study as sold at prevailing prices during the marketing season of the year in which they were raised.

The gross income per plantation increased from $9,974 in 1934 to $13,679 in 1937, an increase of approximately 37 percent for all areas combined (table 20). Significant increases in gross income per plantation were reported in all areas except the Black Belt (B) Area which had a loss of 26 percent (fig. 7 and appendix table 17).

Table 20.—Gross Income From Cash Receipts per Plantation, by Source of Income, 1937 and 1934 [1]

Source of income	Cash receipts per plantation			
	1937		1934	
	Amount	Percent	Amount	Percent
Total	$13, 679	100. 0	$9, 974	100. 0
Crop sales	11, 829	86. 5	8, 342	83. 6
Cotton	10, 721	78. 4	7, 437	74. 5
Feed	194	1. 4	189	1. 9
Other crops	914	6. 7	716	7. 2
AAA payments	1, 237	0. 0	1, 123	11. 3
Livestock products sales	435	3. 2	230	2. 3
Other receipts	178	1. 3	279	2. 8

[1] For data by areas see appendix table 17.

Crop sales accounted for approximately 85 percent of the gross cash receipts per plantation for all areas studied for both crop years and ranged from 75 to 90 percent in the different areas. The predominant position of the cotton enterprise (sale of lint cotton and cottonseed) in plantation income is shown by the fact that operators in only one area, the Atlantic Coast Plain, reported that less than 50 percent of the total cash receipts were from cotton (appendix table 17). Cash receipts from this source ranged in all other areas from about 55 to 87 percent during the years surveyed.

Significant increases in the actual cash receipts per plantation derived from the sale of lint cotton and cottonseed were reported in all areas except the Black Belt (B) Area. The proportion of the total gross cash income derived from the cotton enterprise, however, increased only in the Upper Delta, Lower Delta, Interior Plain, Mississippi Bluffs, and Red River Areas. Conversely, small decreases occurred in the other four areas.

The cash income per plantation derived from feed sales was not important in any area, while cash receipts from other crops per plantation appeared significant in only two of the areas studied, the Atlantic Coast Plain and Black Belt (A) Areas. From the sale principally of tobacco and peanuts these areas derived approximately one-half and one-fifth, respectively, of their gross cash incomes per plantation during both crop years.

Fig. 7 – GROSS INCOME FROM CASH RECEIPTS
          PER PLANTATION, BY AREA
          1937 and 1934

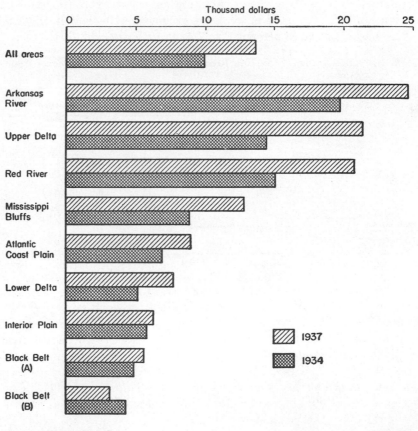

Source: Appendix table 17.   WPA 3310

Benefit payments received under the AAA program ranked second to crops as a source of gross income per plantation. They accounted for 11 percent of the average gross income in 1934 as compared with 9 percent in 1937, although the average amount increased from $1,123 to $1,237. Benefits increased in the majority of areas. In several areas, however, small decreases occurred which were probably due primarily to nonparticipation of some operators in the 1937 program.

Pickers at Work.

Cash sales of livestock products by the plantation operator ranked third as a source of income. A significant upward trend in the sale of livestock products since 1934 had occurred in the majority of areas. Insofar as actual cash income per plantation was concerned though, this source still remained of minor importance in most areas. The future possibilities for expansion of the livestock industry are considerable, however.

Other cash receipts were received chiefly from tenant transactions. Of these the most important was interest on credit advances to tenants for subsistence, seed, and fertilizer while a small amount was received by the operator from commissions through resale of farm products. Cash rent from land and financial returns for special work performed by the operator or under his supervision constituted the smallest source of cash return per plantation. Other cash receipts had declined greatly since 1934, largely because of decreased rental of land by the operator for cash to off-plantation families and the increase in crop acres operated by wage laborers in a number of areas.

A comparison of the 25 percent of the plantations having the highest gross cash income with the 25 percent having the lowest reveals wide differences in the average income per plantation, per family, and per crop acre in each area for both periods studied (appendix table 18). The gross income per plantation for the highest one-fourth was more than double the average income for all plantations in both 1937 and 1934, while the average gross cash income for all plantations was about three and one-half times as large as the income for the lowest one-fourth in both years (tables 21 and 20).

Table 21.—Gross Income for the One-Fourth of the Plantations in Each Area With the Highest and Lowest Gross Income per Plantation, 1937 and 1934 [1]

Item	1937	1934	Percent increase or decrease
Total plantations in each income group	63		
Gross income for one-fourth of plantations with highest gross income per plantation:			
Per plantation	$30,154	$21,322	+41
Per family [2]	982	707	+39
Per crop acre	34	27	+26
Gross income for one-fourth of plantations with lowest gross income per plantation:			
Per plantation	3,715	2,915	+27
Per family [2]	548	395	+39
Per crop acre	21	16	+31

[1] For data by areas see appendix table 18.
[2] Excludes resident families without crops.

Gross income per family for the highest one-fourth was almost 80 percent greater than the comparable gross income for the lowest one-fourth in both years (table 21). On a crop-acre basis income was about

60 to 70 percent higher in the upper than in the lower of these two groups. Gross income per plantation increased more significantly between the two years for plantations in the highest one-fourth than in the lowest one-fourth, the average increases being 41 percent and 27 percent, respectively. Income per family, on the other hand, increased at the same rate for both groups, 39 percent. Returns per crop acre, while remaining much less in the lower than in the upper group, increased relatively more in the lower income group—31 percent as compared with 26 percent for the upper income group.

CURRENT EXPENSES

The operators of plantations of the size covered by this study have heavy current expenses during the production of the crop and for maintenance of the property. Coincident with the expansion of crop acreage and changes in labor practices, the operating costs also rose.

Current expenditures per plantation, exclusive of expenditures for the erection of new buildings, fences, drainage work, and other capital improvements, amounted to $6,006 in 1937 in comparison with $4,285 in 1934 or a 40 percent increase (table 22). Wide differences in expenditures appeared among areas and in the same area from one year to another (appendix table 19). Expenditures per plantation had increased since 1934 in all areas except the Black Belt (B) Area where the decrease was negligible.

Table 22.—Current Expenses per Plantation, 1937 and 1934 [1]

Item	1937	1934
Total plantations	246	
Current expenses per plantation	$6,006	$4,285
Labor	2,166	1,319
Regular wage laborers [2]	658	631
Seasonal wage laborers	1,037	226
Cotton chopping	120	85
Cotton picking	917	141
Tenant occasional	364	296
Miscellaneous	107	166
Other crop expenses	2,468	1,835
Feed and veterinary fees	107	229
Seed, fertilizer, and poison for pest control	793	633
Tractor expenses	197	130
Ginning	1,065	551
Rent	306	292
Repairs	497	342
Real estate	605	613
Insurance	119	106
Taxes	486	507
Interest	211	122
Miscellaneous	59	54

[1] For data by areas see appendix table 19.
[2] Includes nonresident laborers.

For all areas combined, wages for labor constituted approximately 36 percent of the total expenditures per plantation in 1937 as compared with about 31 percent in 1934. Every area studied, with the exception of the two Black Belt areas, showed a significant increase in expenditures for labor. While regular wage laborer expenditures had increased since 1934 in the majority of the areas studied, this type of expenditure had been reduced by more than 50 percent in the Red River and Arkansas River Areas. Seasonal labor expenditures for all areas were between four and five times as large in 1937 as in 1934 with the increases concentrated in the western areas. The increases were due largely to expanded acreage in cotton and to high cotton yields in 1937 as compared with 1934. Tenant occasional labor was also used to a greater extent in 1937 than in 1934 in most areas for the same reasons. Some plantation operators use tenant occasional labor only, while others use this group together with off-plantation labor for all cropping practices.

Other crop expenses accounted for approximately 41 percent of the total expenditures per plantation for all areas in 1937 and a slightly higher percent in 1934. Ginning, the largest of such expenses per plantation in 1937, together with seed and fertilizer costs, accounted for the major portion of other crop expenditures in both years. Improved (and hence more expensive) seed in 1937 as compared with 1934 and use of greater amounts of fertilizer were other factors in the increased crop expenses.

Repairs to buildings, fences, and implements had also mounted since 1934 in most areas. Less than one-third as much was spent for this item in the Interior Plain Area, however, in 1937 as in 1934. Insurance on plantation property had increased in most areas. Taxes per plantation were slightly reduced for all areas combined, while major reductions had occurred in the Red River Area.

Interest as here discussed applies only to money borrowed for plantation farming operations in the crop years 1937 and 1934. Between the two years this item rose by 73 percent for all plantations studied. Only two areas, the Black Belt (A) and Mississippi Bluffs Areas, had reduced the interest cost during the period covered.

PLANTATION NET CASH INCOME

To obtain plantation net cash income, current expenses of both the operator and tenants were subtracted from the total plantation gross income. The items deducted included expenditures for feed, seed, and fertilizer; interest on short-term loans; labor; current repairs to plantation buildings, fences, and implements; insurance and taxes; and other current cash expenditures. Costs chargeable to depreciation, improvements, and interest on long-term credit were not included.

The net cash income per plantation increased from $5,689 in 1934 to $7,673 in 1937 or 35 percent (table 23 and fig. 8). All areas showed

Table 23.—Net Cash Income per Plantation and per Crop Acre, by Area, 1937 and 1934

Area	Total plan- tations	Net cash income			
		Per plantation		Per crop acre	
		1937	1934	1937	1934
All areas	246	$7,673	$5,689	$16	$14
Atlantic Coast Plain	31	5,589	4,449	17	18
Black Belt (A)	31	2,915	2,620	8	9
Black Belt (B)	16	918	2,004	4	8
Upper Delta	79	11,740	8,071	20	15
Lower Delta	19	4,703	3,653	13	15
Interior Plain	17	3,941	3,478	10	10
Mississippi Bluffs	27	8,020	5,282	18	13
Red River	15	10,021	6,830	14	13
Arkansas River	11	14,403	12,458	15	14

Fig. 8 – NET CASH INCOME PER PLANTATION, BY AREA
1937 and 1934

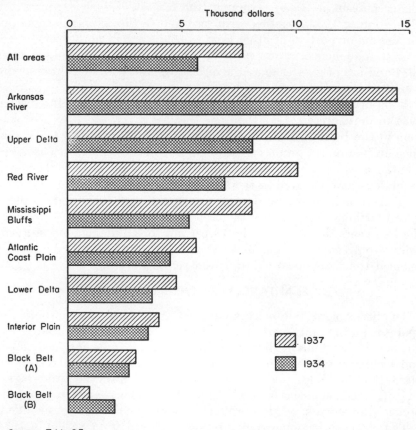

Source: Table 23.

WPA 3319

Weighing Up.

increases in cash earnings since 1934 with the exception of the Black Belt (B) Area in which the net income per plantation was less than one-half as large in 1937 as in 1934. Factors responsible for higher net cash incomes were increased crop acreage planted to cotton and exceptionally high yields, which more than compensated for the decline in prices between the two years.

Net cash income per crop acre increased in only four of the nine areas. While it declined most markedly in the Black Belt (B) Area, decreases also occurred in the Atlantic Coast Plain, Black Belt (A) and Lower Delta Areas and no change occurred in the Interior Plain Area.[1]

---

[1] For a financial summary of plantation operations see appendix table 20.

Chapter V

OPERATOR AND TENANT INCOME

THE COMPLEX internal organization and operation of plantations, together with wide variations among individual units, present difficult problems in measuring the net earnings of operator and tenant. Data analyzed in this chapter are for cash income only, as the value of products used for home consumption was not obtained on the 1937 schedules.[1]

OPERATOR'S CASH INCOME

As far as the individual operator is concerned, the success of the year's plantation operation is determined primarily by whether or not he himself receives a satisfactory net cash income after deduction of current expenses from his gross income.

Gross Cash Income

The gross income of the operator for a given year is, to a large extent, a reflection of acreage in crops and especially of the proportion planted to cotton together with the average yield per acre and the price level of the money crop. In addition, the type of labor or combinations of labor types used on the plantation affect the gross returns as some prove more efficient than others. Another factor is the variations in the management ability of the operators. After sale of the crop the operator retains his share of the cropper and share tenant crop plus the amounts advanced for subsistence and production expenses and the interest on such advances. The total proceeds from acreage operated by wage labor are retained by the operator. In acting as the marketing agent, the operator may exercise his prerogative by selling the product at once or holding part or all of the

---

[1] In 1934 home-use production amounted to an average of $32 for wage laborers, $105 for croppers, $145 for share tenants, and $158 for renters.

crop for speculative purposes. In either case he credits the tenants' accounts for the product at prevailing market prices at the time of settling in the autumn, making the deductions specified above.

The operator may rent acreage in addition to owned acreage or he may rent out part or all of his acreage. In either case the proceeds received are considered as operator rather than plantation income. Furthermore, the operator's income is augmented by benefits which he receives for participation in the Agricultural Adjustment Administration program and by the sale of livestock products.

For all areas the average gross cash income of the operator increased from $5,908 in 1934 to $8,328 in 1937 or approximately 41 percent (table 24). Significant increases were found in most areas, and only in the Black Belt (B) Area was the average gross income less in 1937 than in 1934 (appendix table 21). Approximately 83 percent of the operator's income in 1937 was obtained from crop sales as compared with 75 percent in 1934. Although their proportionate importance differed considerably from area to area, crop sales provided the primary source of income in all areas.

Table 24.—Operator's Gross Cash Income From Cash Receipts per Plantation, by Source of Income, 1937 and 1934 [1]

Source of income	Gross cash income per plantation	
	1937	1934
Total	$8,328	$5,908
Crop sales	6,882	4,420
AAA payments	833	979
Livestock products sales	435	230
Other receipts [2]	178	279

[1] For data by areas see appendix table 21.
[2] Cash rent, interest, commissions, and miscellaneous.

Next to crop sales, payments for participation in the AAA program contributed the largest income in 1937 in all areas except the Black Belt (A) Area in which income from the sale of livestock products was more important. Although income derived from the sale of livestock products was not significant in most areas in either year studied, this source is gradually increasing in importance. Income from other sources was not large in either year and was even less important in 1937 than in 1934. Reductions were due especially to decreased income from land rental, lower interest rates, and a slight decline in commissions.

Current Expenses

Significant increases in the operator's current plantation expenditures for the crop year 1937 over 1934 were found in the majority of the areas studied (table 25 and fig. 9), although only a slight increase was noted in the Black Belt (B) Area and a slight reduction in the Interior Plain Area. Current expenses per plantation in 1937 ranged from $1,889 in the Interior Plain Area to $9,681 in the Red River Area.

Table 25.—Operator's Current Expenses per Plantation, by Area, 1937 and 1934

Area	Total plantations	Current expenses per plantation	
		1937	1934
All areas	246	$4,738	$3,380
Atlantic Coast Plain	31	2,931	2,087
Black Belt (A)	31	2,049	1,786
Black Belt (B)	16	1,915	1,894
Upper Delta	79	7,293	4,862
Lower Delta	19	2,145	1,154
Interior Plain	17	1,889	1,968
Mississippi Bluffs	27	3,472	2,204
Red River	15	9,681	7,743
Arkansas River	11	9,382	6,382

Net Cash Income

The net cash income of the operator was obtained by deducting current expenses from gross cash income. The average net cash income of all operators surveyed rose from $2,528 in 1934 to $3,590 in 1937 or 42 percent (table 26 and fig. 9). Only the Atlantic Coast Plain and the two Black Belt Areas failed to show increases. A severe decline occurred in the Black Belt (B) Area in which the average was reduced from $1,113 to $215.

Table 26.—Operator's Net Cash Income per Plantation, by Area, 1937 and 1934

Area	Total plantations	Net cash income per plantation	
		1937	1934
All areas	246	$3,590	$2,528
Atlantic Coast Plain	31	1,906	2,170
Black Belt (A)	31	1,378	1,433
Black Belt (B)	16	215	1,113
Upper Delta	79	5,616	3,278
Lower Delta	19	2,422	1,816
Interior Plain	17	1,770	1,558
Mississippi Bluffs	27	4,124	2,420
Red River	15	4,598	2,796
Arkansas River	11	7,826	6,409

Net Cash Gain or Loss

Within the period under study less than 10 percent of the total operators reported actual losses in their plantation enterprises (appendix table 22). The majority of those with losses reported net cash

Fig. 9 — CASH INCOME* PER OPERATOR, BY AREA
    1937 and 1934

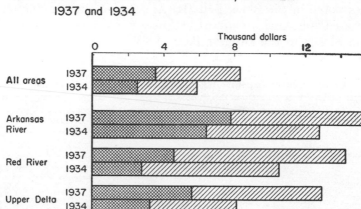

* Total length of bar equals gross cash income.

Source: Appendix table 23.

WPA 3312

losses of less than $500. In fact for this group with small losses the average loss in 1937 was $144 and in 1934, $212. The seven operators with heavy losses in 1934 averaged a net loss of $869. The corresponding losses for eight operators in 1937 averaged $1,636.

For the operators who reported actual net cash returns from their plantation enterprises the average earnings were $4,331 in 1937 as compared with $2,996 in 1934, a gain of 45 percent. The increase in the average net cash gain per operator for the crop year 1937 is indicated by the fact that 27 percent received $5,000 or more and averaged $10,268 as compared with 15 percent and an average income of $9,362 for 1934. Moreover, only 23 percent of the operators reported a net gain of less than $1,000 in 1937 as contrasted with 29

Loading for the Gin.

percent in 1934.   Thus, data on operator's net gain or loss substantiate the conclusion that the economic situation of plantations in the Southeast was far better in the good cotton year 1937 than it had been in 1934.[2]

The operator's net cash income, however, represents the return for his supervisory labor and interest on his invested capital.   Deducting a 6 percent return on invested capital, operator labor income was $645 in 1934 as compared with $1,340 in 1937.   In both years the labor income was much below the earnings the average operator would have been expected to receive from another occupation.

TENANT'S CASH INCOME

The analysis of tenant income has been limited to sharecroppers and share tenants.   Renters (cash and standing) were relatively few in number on the plantations surveyed and were a more independent group, receiving little or no supervision and exercising much the same prerogatives as owner-operators.   Croppers and share tenants on plantations, on the other hand, are usually supervised as closely in their work as are wage laborers; in addition, they are dependent on the operator for production expenses and subsistence.

Gross Cash Income

Gross cash income includes the value of the tenant's share of the crops produced, payments received from the AAA, and wages for labor.   In the present study only earnings from plantation labor were reported.

The average gross cash income per tenant family for all areas increased from $331 in 1934 to $385 in 1937 or approximately 16 percent (table 27).   Moreover, tenants in all areas had increases in average gross earnings except those in the Interior Plain Area where a slight decline occurred and in the Black Belt (B) Area where a decline of about 20 percent was reported.   The variations in average gross income reflected principally changes in the cotton enterprise, for other sources produced relatively little income except in the Atlantic Coast Plain Area where about 50 percent of the average tenant income from crop sales was from tobacco.   Variations in income from the cotton enterprise were caused by changes in acreage and production of cotton and in payments received for participation in the AAA program.

The returns from plantation occasional labor, in which the tenant worked on the plantation but not on his own acreage, averaged about $25 per year.   This source of income was of importance only in the

---

[2] For a summary of the operator's financial situation see appendix table 23.

Red River Area where tenants reported $118 in earnings, on the average, for 1937.

Current Expenses

The major item in current expenses was advances for subsistence plus interest which averaged over $100 in both 1934 and 1937. The amount declined slightly for all areas combined between the two years, although the majority of individual areas had slight increases (table 27). The principal crop expenses incurred by the tenant were for ginning, fertilizer, labor for cotton picking and other cropping practices, supervision, and interest. As a result of increases in acreage, volume of production, and the cost of individual items, crop expenses rose slightly in most of the areas studied. For all areas combined they increased from $68 to $85 per tenant.

Table 27.—Net Income [1] per Tenant Family,[2] by Area, 1937 and 1934

Area	Total families reporting	Gross cash income				Crop expenses [4]	Subsistence advances [5]	Cash after settling	Net income
		Total	Crop sales	AAA payments	Labor [3]				
All areas:									
1937	3,272	$385	[6] $331	$27	$27	$85	$104	$196	$300
1934	3,003	331	[7] 296	11	24	68	112	151	263
Atlantic Coast Plain:									
1937	164	635	[8] 570	29	36	70	136	429	565
1934	145	517	[9] 487	21	9	68	116	333	449
Black Belt (A):									
1937	166	336	[10] 308	14	14	91	95	150	245
1934	160	312	[11] 290	9	13	84	88	140	228
Black Belt (B):									
1937	67	265	216	22	27	60	138	67	205
1934	62	333	308	9	16	87	99	147	246
Upper Delta:									
1937	1,576	405	372	18	15	106	109	190	299
1934	1,453	365	320	11	34	81	121	163	284
Lower Delta:									
1937	249	215	206	8	1	58	78	79	157
1934	184	165	161	3	1	24	91	50	141
Interior Plain:									
1937	108	362	272	63	27	53	91	218	309
1934	113	385	323	15	47	49	161	175	336
Mississippi Bluffs:									
1937	386	380	322	42	16	98	107	175	282
1934	373	291	273	10	8	91	92	108	200
Red River:									
1937	234	451	292	41	118	55	82	314	396
1934	198	271	244	9	18	29	119	123	242
Arkansas River:									
1937	322	311	204	51	56	30	99	182	281
1934	315	263	233	10	20	32	96	135	231

[1] Excludes home-use production.
[2] Cropper and share tenant families only.
[3] Average earnings per tenant family for plantation occasional labor.
[4] Seed, feed, fertilizer, labor, etc.
[5] Subsistence advances plus interest. This total will not check with data in table 18 as average current expenses for subsistence are based on all tenant families, including those not receiving subsistence advances.
[6] Tobacco and peanuts accounted for 6 percent of the total.
[7] Tobacco and peanuts accounted for 5 percent of the total.
[8] Tobacco accounted for 55 percent of the total.
[9] Tobacco accounted for 47 percent of the total.
[10] Tobacco and peanuts accounted for 20 percent of the total.
[11] Tobacco and peanuts accounted for 21 percent of the total.

Net Cash Income

The net cash income per tenant family after settling with the landlord rose from $151 in 1934 to $196 in 1937 or about 30 percent (table 27). Although wide differences in income occurred from area to area, significant increases since 1934 were general. The average for the Black Belt (B) Area, however, declined from $147 to $67. The highest cash income per family was reported in the Atlantic Coast Plain Area and was due to the dependence on tobacco. Among the areas dependent on cotton the highest average net cash income in 1937 was $314 in the Red River Area. Of this total $118 was from wages for plantation labor.

The average net cash income after settling of croppers on plantations which had this type of tenant exclusively rose from $137 in 1934 to $216 in 1937 (table 28). This resulted from increases in cotton acreage and yield in addition to an increase in income from working at occasional plantation labor. In both years income per cropper family was considerably higher in the Atlantic Coast Plain Area than in other areas because of high cash returns from tobacco in addition to cotton. The croppers in the Red River Area had experienced the greatest actual increase since 1934, partly because of definitely higher earnings in 1937 from plantation occasional labor.

Table 28.—Net Cash Income [1] per Cropper Family,[2] by Area, 1937 and 1934

Area	Total families reporting		Net cash income per cropper family	
	1937	1934	1937	1934
All areas	1,620	1,281	$216	$137
Atlantic Coast Plain	123	127	490	362
Black Belt (A)	149	128	171	152
Black Belt (B)	62	29	38	102
Upper Delta	576	510	208	115
Lower Delta	143	36	90	17
Interior Plain	46	90	154	104
Mississippi Bluffs	190	164	153	94
Red River	218	154	323	122
Arkansas River	113	43	231	121

[1] After settling with the landlord. Excludes subsistence advances and home-use production.
[2] Based on plantations operated by croppers only.

In comparison with croppers, share tenants on plantations operated exclusively by this type of labor had lower net cash incomes in both years studied. They averaged only $103 in 1934 and $187 in 1937.[3]

Net Cash Income by Cotton Acreage

Variations in tenant net cash income are directly related to crop acres operated, especially to the proportion of the acreage planted to

[3] Data on file in the Division of Research, Work Projects Administration, Washington, D. C.

the major cash crop—cotton.[4] Croppers and share tenants having from 50 to 70 percent of their total crop acres in cotton in 1937 received the highest median net cash income, $309 as compared with $220 for all tenants (appendix table 24). Relatively little difference was found in the median cash income of tenants having 30 to 50 percent or over 70 percent of their crop acreage in cotton and the median income for all tenants in 1937. Tenants with less than 30 percent of their total crop acres in cotton had the lowest median cash income in 1937, whereas tenants having less than 30 percent of their crop acres in cotton in 1934 received the same median income as those tenants having 30 to 70 percent of their acreage in cotton. The tenants having 70 percent or more of their crop acres planted to cotton in that year received the highest median cash income which was only slightly above the average for all tenants in 1937. Thus, the variations in net cash income on the basis of proportion of crop acreage in cotton were found to be much greater in 1937 than in 1934.

Net Income

After deducting expenses for actual crop production, the net income of croppers and share tenants combined, exclusive of home-use production, rose from $263 in 1934 to $300 in 1937 (table 27). Of these totals, $112 was for subsistence advances and $151 for net cash income after settling in 1934 and $104 was for subsistence advances and $196 for net cash income in 1937. If an estimated $100 for production for home use is added to crop income and subsistence, the total net income of croppers and share tenants combined is found to have averaged only about $400 even in the good cotton year of 1937. On the basis of such low incomes it is clearly impossible for the average tenant to raise his level of living above mere subsistence or to accumulate resources with which to improve his tenure status. Moreover, because of his precarious economic position, he readily falls a victim to any change in agricultural practices. The importance of this fact has been clearly demonstrated by the large-scale relief needs in rural areas of the South during the past few years.

---

[4] In the Atlantic Coast Plain Area tobacco was the major cash crop. See table 27.

Mechanical Cotton Picker at Work.

Chapter VI

RELIEF NEEDS IN THE SOUTH

ONLY THROUGH an understanding of the factors which make for recurring periods of prosperity and depression for the farmer can a sound program for attacking human dependency in the South be developed. The first five chapters of this report are limited to a single segment of Southern agriculture, that associated with the larger, more efficient production units in cotton counties of the South-east. The facts as to this segment indicate that its economy has partially recovered from the extreme disorganization of the early 1930's. Operators are earning a return on their capital and a small additional labor income. Tenants" incomes, while extremely low, suffice to keep them from going on relief. However, fewer tenant families per 1,000 crop acres are participating in this economy than formerly.

Interspersed with the plantations are thousands of smaller units occupying less fertile land and producing smaller yields per acre. The income picture for the operators of these units is less favorable than for plantation operators except where they depend to a larger degree on home-use production.

On both the large and the small units the reduced demand for cotton and the increased efficiency in production have displaced workers to the extent that there are now fewer people participating in the profits from the cotton economy than there were in the 1920's. Still another consideration is the fact that the oncoming generation of new workers is far larger than can be absorbed in such a situation. At the same time these workers who cannot find places in agriculture do not have adequate opportunities for employment in other industries.

POPULATION TRENDS

More than one-half (53 percent on January 1, 1935) of the farm population of the Nation is in the South,[1] and the basic causes of Southern relief problems are to be found in the maladjustments of this farm population in relation to agricultural opportunity and in its pressure toward the towns and villages where it cannot be absorbed. Southern farm families furnish over one-fourth of the total increase in the Nation's labor supply, or more than 200,000 annually during the 1930's.

Normally, there is a flow of maturing laborers from farm to non-farm areas and from the South to other sections, but during the early years of the depression the net movement from farms was cut to one-fifth of its usual volume.[2] The estimates of the Bureau of Agricultural Economics indicate a net shift from farms in the South to villages, towns, and cities of more than 105,000 persons per year from 1930 through 1934 or almost as much as the national total of approximately 120,000. Even so, this net shift of some 525,000 from Southern farms in the years 1930–1934 did not drain off the natural increase of 736,000 in the Southern farm population. This increase was largely concentrated in the Appalachian-Ozark and other part-time farming areas, while the farm population of the cotton areas remained about constant. There were important shifts within this population, however. The fact that the persons of working age were banking up in the population is indicated by the increase in unpaid family laborers shown by the 1935 Census.

CHANGE IN NUMBER OF FARM OPERATORS, 1930 TO 1935

Southern agriculture in the early depression years, especially in 1931 and 1932, was so disorganized that many farmers were forced out of agriculture entirely, while many tenants were forced into the labor class and many farm laborers were displaced. The years 1933 and 1934 were years of partial recovery so that comparison of census figures for 1930 and 1935 shows the results of the slump and partial recovery.

For the purposes of this discussion the mountain areas and border South are not included because, while the farm problems of these sections are serious, they are of a special character pertaining to subsistence and part-time farming. Hence the statistics on changes in

---

[1] Alabama, Arkansas, Delaware, Florida, Georgia, Kentucky, Louisiana, Maryland, Mississippi, North Carolina, Oklahoma, South Carolina, Tennessee, Texas, Virginia, and West Virginia. See Bureau of the Census, *United States Census of Agriculture: 1935*, Vol. III, U. S. Department of Commerce, Washington, D. C., 1937, p. 144.

[2] Bureau of Agricultural Economics, *Farm Population Estimates, January 1, 1939*, U. S. Department of Agriculture, Washington, D. C., June 22, 1939, p. 7.

numbers and types of farms are confined primarily to the cotton regions of the Old South. In these regions the total number of farms reported by the census remained almost constant from 1930 to 1935 (table 29), slight increases in the Southeast being offset by slight decreases in the Mississippi Delta and central Texas.[3] The Southeastern increases were probably not cotton farms as many were in suburban areas around cities and in the Upper Piedmont textile area.

Table 29.—Changes in Farm Population and in Farm Operators in Southern Regions, [1] 1930 to 1935

Item	April 1, 1930	January 1, 1935	Change
FARM POPULATION			
Total	16, 191, 000	16, 927, 000	+736, 000
Cotton regions [2]	10, 333, 000	10, 302, 000	−31, 000
Noncotton regions	5, 858, 000	6, 625, 000	+767, 000
FARM OPERATORS			
Total	3, 224, 000	3, 422, 000	+198, 000
Cotton regions [2]	2, 066, 000	2, 077, 000	+11, 000
Noncotton regions	1, 158, 000	1, 345, 000	+187, 000

[1] Includes Alabama, Arkansas, Delaware, Florida, Georgia, Kentucky, Louisiana, Maryland, Mississippi, North Carolina, Oklahoma, South Carolina, Tennessee, Texas, Virginia, and West Virginia.
[2] East Central Oklahoma, Eastern Old South, Mississippi Delta, and Western Old South Regions and adjacent subregions as delimited by Mangus, A. R., *Rural Regions of the United States*, Division of Research, Work Projects Administration, Washington, D. C., 1940.

Source: Bureau of the Census, *United States Census of Agriculture: 1935*, Vols. I and II, U. S. Department of Commerce, Washington, D. C., 1936.

A considerable shifting of status occurred within the farm population. Owners and managers increased by 54,000 (table 30). This was partly the result of an increase in subsistence and part-time farmers. Tenants (other than croppers) increased by 20,000. This was in a large measure an increase in displaced tenants, i. e., those still living on farms and operating as much as 3 acres in a desultory way but without a cotton crop or the usual landlord-tenant agreement. Croppers showed a decrease of 63,000 or nearly 10 percent.

Table 30.—Changes in Farm Operators in Southern Cotton Regions,[1] by Tenure, 1930 to 1935

Item	Total	Owners and managers	Tenants	Croppers
1930	2, 066, 000	695, 000	715, 000	656, 000
1935	2, 077, 000	749, 000	735, 000	593, 000
Change	+11, 000	+54, 000	+20, 000	−63, 000

[1] East Central Oklahoma, Eastern Old South, Mississippi Delta, and Western Old South Regions and adjacent subregions as delimited by Mangus, A. R., *Rural Regions of the United States*, Division of Research, Work Projects Administration, Washington, D. C., 1940.

Source: Bureau of the Census, *United States Census of Agriculture: 1935*, Vol. I, U. S. Department of Commerce, Washington, D. C., 1936.

[3] Turner, H. A., *A Graphic Summary of Farm Tenure*, Miscellaneous Publication No. 261, U. S. Department of Agriculture, Washington, D. C., 1936, pp. 24–25.

The registration in the Unemployment Census of November 1937 was far under the total number of unemployed.[4] Nevertheless, one fact about the South was clear: namely, that unemployment[5] among farm operators and farm laborers was more frequent in the South than in other sections. It was even more frequent than in the Great Plains drought section. Of the Southern registrants reporting occupations 6 percent were farm operators as compared with 3 percent in the whole country. Twenty-four percent were farm laborers as against twelve percent for the whole country.[6]

All of these data point to the existence of a huge needy farm population. It is difficult to express this need in numbers because its volume varies from year to year and even from month to month with the fortunes of agriculture and because it differs under varying definitions of need. It seems likely, however, that in 1938 there were at least 1,200,000 displaced farmers, excess youth remaining on farms, and displaced farm laborers in the South who were in need of public assistance.

In addition to these groups which have a farm background but are more or less detached from productive agriculture, the operation of the plantation system creates a situation in which many of the tenants and small owners desperately need a cash income during the winter months. Ordinarily planters furnish their tenants with subsistence advances for 7 or 8 months. Since these advances are secured by the growing crop, they usually do not start until the crop is planted and stop when it is sold. Moreover, the amount of credit is largely dependent upon the expected value of the tenant's share of the crop. A study of 646 plantations in 1934 showed the average duration of tenant advances to be 6.9 months and the average monthly advance to be $12.50.[7] Thus the tenant is usually on his own resources for 5 winter months—October, November, December, January, and February. He is virtually unemployed in agriculture during this time, just as workers in seasonal industries have periods of unemployment. Before the depression farmers who did not clear enough on their crops to get through the winter depended on odd jobs, clearing land, hauling wood, etc., to pick up the necessary cash. During the

---

[4] Census of Partial Employment, Unemployment, and Occupations: 1937, *Final Report on Total and Partial Unemployment*, Vol. IV, Washington, D. C., 1938, pp. 5–8.

[5] Including persons totally and partially unemployed and engaged in emergency work in 16 Southern States.

[6] Census of Partial Employment, Unemployment, and Occupations: 1937, *op. cit.*, Vol. I, pp. 74, 77, and 80.

[7] Woofter, T. J., Jr. and Others, *Landlord and Tenant on the Cotton Plantation*, Research Monograph V, Division of Social Research, Works Progress Administration, Washington, D. C., 1936, p. 59.

depression, for various reasons, these opportunities for winter employment have virtually disappeared. Lumbering is at a low ebb; planters do not do as much clearing of new land as formerly; and public construction, financed by counties and towns, is far below predepression levels.

In order to understand this winter need it is necessary to examine the disposal of the cropper's income. According to the 1934 study, the cropper's income averaged (with 12-cent cotton) $312, of which $105 was in home-use production, most of which was used during the summer and fall.[8] An average of $21 was earned by work away from his own farm. His cash crop brought $186, but he had drawn $85 in subsistence advances during the crop season so he received only $101 in cash at the end of the year. This was about $20 a month to tide him over the 5 months during which no advances were available and to buy his annual supply of clothing and pay off such items as doctors' bills.

It must be remembered that this is an average figure and that thousands below the average had less than this amount on which to get through the winter. In fact, on 14 percent of the plantations, even with 12-cent cotton, cropper and other share tenant net incomes were less than $200, including home-use products.[9] In 1938, with 8-cent cotton, the proportion of such tenants having less than an adequate amount of money to carry them through the winter was at least 35 percent of the total or from 350,000 to 400,000.

EXTENT OF FEDERAL AID

On a per capita basis the South has not received as much Federal aid as most other sections, partly because it is dominantly rural and rural groups have been less articulate than urban groups about their needs, partly because living standards are so low that standards of acceptance for relief have been lower than in other sections, and partly because, for the same reason, amounts of relief granted per case have been relatively lower than in other sections.

The accompanying map shows per capita Federal aid under the combined FERA, CWA, Resettlement-Farm Security, and WPA programs cumulated from January 1933 through March 1938 (fig. 10). High per capita expenditures in the Plains States, where drought conditions have been serious in recent years, are in contrast to very low per capita expenditures in the South. In the cotton States per capita expenditures have ranged from $24 to $59; in the Plains States, from $49 to $116 (table 31).

---

[8] *Ibid.*, p. 87.
[9] *Ibid.*, p. 222.

Fig. 10 - FEDERAL AID PER CAPITA*

January 1933 - March 1938

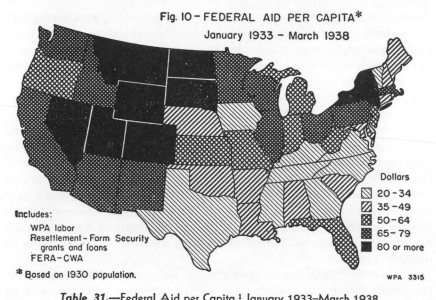

Dollars

▨ 20-34
▨ 35-49
▨ 50-64
▨ 65-79
■ 80 or more

Includes:
WPA labor
Resettlement - Farm Security
grants and loans
FERA - CWA

* Based on 1930 population.

WPA 3315

Table 31.—Federal Aid per Capita,[1] January 1933–March 1938

[12 Southern and 7 drought States]

State	Total	WPA labor	Resettlement-Farm Security grants and loans	FERA-CWA	Aid per capita
SOUTHERN STATES					
Total	$1,117,361,317	$385,561,354	$83,570,876	$648,229,087	$35.86
Alabama	96,867,758	30,210,548	7,314,483	59,342,727	36.61
Arkansas	83,490,255	25,500,434	7,387,845	50,601,976	45.02
Florida	85,946,209	28,852,396	3,481,837	53,611,976	58.54
Georgia	100,068,822	33,065,234	7,150,942	59,852,646	34.41
Louisiana	104,457,422	37,947,633	5,444,761	61,065,028	49.70
Mississippi	66,614,880	21,991,106	7,265,792	37,357,982	33.14
North Carolina	75,081,104	23,498,022	4,354,100	47,228,982	23.68
Oklahoma	115,075,633	49,394,573	12,100,061	53,580,999	48.03
South Carolina	69,924,979	21,873,380	5,344,394	42,707,205	40.22
Tennessee	75,501,548	27,736,237	2,104,405	45,660,906	28.86
Texas	185,321,339	62,491,621	19,127,077	103,702,641	31.82
Virginia	59,011,368	23,000,170	2,495,179	33,516,019	24.37
DROUGHT STATES					
Total	471,125,693	180,408,073	77,645,964	213,071,656	73.25
Colorado	88,342,379	39,405,748	7,193,794	41,742,837	85.29
Kansas	98,587,383	41,620,976	12,006,939	44,959,468	52.41
Montana	54,192,298	21,022,423	5,414,300	27,755,575	100.80
Nebraska	67,593,531	28,429,319	12,219,321	26,944,891	49.05
North Dakota	63,848,193	20,703,234	17,359,267	25,785,692	93.78
South Dakota	80,314,871	23,782,182	20,176,413	36,356,276	115.92
Wyoming	18,247,038	5,444,191	3,275,930	9,526,917	80.89

[1] Based on 1930 population.

Relief loads have varied considerably in different sections of the South. The proportion of families on relief in the Appalachian counties has remained high throughout the depression. In the cotton counties relief loads were heavy in 1933 and 1934 and dropped rapidly in 1935, 1936, and early 1937 to mount again in late 1937 and 1938. According to standards existing in other sections of the country much need still existed in 1935, 1936, and 1937, but owing to restrictions on quotas, lack of funds, and the limitation of State funds for general relief not all of this need was met. The expansion of programs in 1938 represented an effort both to meet previous need and to care for the increase in number of needy families as a result of the economic recession of that year.

In November 1936 the combined Works Progress Administration, Resettlement Administration, and general relief loads were 966,000 or more than 311,000 under the November 1933 level (table 32). By November 1937 (a low point) there was a further drop to 730,000 in the combined load. From November 1937 to November 1938 the expansion was rapid. WPA increased its employment to 873,000 or over 140 percent. General relief rose slightly and the Farm Security Administration, replacing the Resettlement Administration, decreased its loan and grant load from 250,000 to 193,000. The combined total again amounted to well over a million cases and approximated the November 1933 general relief load. About 175,000 of the WPA increase was due to the change of policy made in August 1938 to give between-season employment to needy farmers.

Table 32.—Households Receiving Public Assistance [1] in the South,[2] November 1933–November 1938

Month and year	General relief	WPA	Resettlement-Farm Security grants and loans
November 1933	1,276,838	—	—
May 1934	1,211,879	—	—
November 1934	1,307,110	—	—
May 1935	1,179,142	—	—
November 1935	734,998	656,403	—
May 1936	227,755	557,561	—
November 1936	177,366	593,246	195,305
May 1937	170,656	481,516	252,619
November 1937	117,628	361,574	250,471
May 1938	148,324	616,632	204,177
November 1938	135,561	872,507	192,555

[1] Excluding Social Security classes, the Civilian Conservation Corps, and the National Youth Administration.
[2] Alabama, Arkansas, Delaware, Florida, Georgia, Kentucky, Louisiana, Maryland, Mississippi, North Carolina, Oklahoma, South Carolina, Tennessee, Texas, Virginia, and West Virginia.

Among the cases aided in the South in November 1938, it is estimated that 600,000 included employable workers with farm backgrounds. The rate at which WPA applications were increasing in December and January is evidence of the great volume of need and there appears to be no immediate probability of its reduction. In November 1938 in addition to the agricultural workers employed by WPA there were approximately 400,000 persons with farm backgrounds eligible and certified for employment who could not be given employment under the existing quotas, and the number was being steadily increased by applications to public welfare offices.

If all families earning less than $312 per year in cash are considered eligible for public assistance, nearly a million and a half families with rural backgrounds may be applicants. If a stricter criterion is used and only those detached from agriculture and earning less than about $200 are included, somewhere in the neighborhood of a million farm families may be expected to apply if unemployed youth, many of whom are secondary workers in the household, are included as eligible. But whatever criterion is used, the number of needy is stupendous and offers convincing proof of the inadequacy of present programs to cope completely with the widespread destitution in the rural South.

Chapter VII

LIVING CONDITIONS

PRECEDING CHAPTERS have shown that the Southern cotton planter was in a far better position economically in 1937 than 3 years previously. His tenants likewise had experienced some improvement as reflected in net cash income, but they still were unable to provide living conditions for themselves and their families which would meet minimum requirements for the so-called American standard of living. In addition, relief loads were large, but provisions for public assistance were still inadequate to care for added thousands upon thousands of needy rural families in the South. Conditions described in this chapter apply not only to the less secure among the plantation families but also to the great numbers of other rural families in the South whose existence is marked by poverty and deprivation. The problems are not new, but additional data on diet, housing, health, education, and plane of living as they become available serve to throw the situation into ever sharper relief.

DIET

Inadequate nutrition constitutes a basic problem in the South. The meager diets generally found among low-income farm families in this section result not only from lack of money with which to purchase a variety of foodstuffs but also from ignorance and from food habits of long standing. Gardens are primarily seasonal in character and poorly tended, while canning and storing of food are usually at a minimum among the group which most needs these types of provision for winter diet. Lack of supplies, canning equipment, and refrigeration are frequently major obstacles to food preservation.

While the traditional corn meal, fat pork, and molasses of the Cotton Belt are now generally supplemented by refined wheat flour and sugar,[1] such changes have actually decreased the nutritional value of the basic diet. Unless they raise the products themselves, the poorer farm families are unable to supplement this diet with the needed quantities of milk, eggs, vegetables, fruits, and lean meat. Hence the adequacy of the diet is directly dependent upon production for home use.[2]

Persons who are familiar with the large and carefully tended gardens of other agricultural sections often do not realize that it is not simply inertia which prevents the sharecropper or farm laborer from raising much of his own food. He needs land and seed; he needs encouragement and education to change the agricultural practices of decades; he needs to be taught the importance of improving the diet of his family. Meanwhile, if attached to a plantation, he knows that the landlord will furnish subsistence and that he can live on credit during the growing season as he has always done. As the advances average less than $15 per month and families are large, however, a diet meeting nutritional standards cannot be provided.

In a recent survey of 697 rural families, predominantly farm and open country nonfarm, at the bottom of the economic ladder in 5 counties in the South,[3] the families were asked how many days during the past week their diet had included 5 common items—pork, eggs, milk, butter, and beef (table 33). The results were little short of appalling and indicate that the poverty-stricken rural family is little better off dietetically today than it was 30 years ago.[4]

In Hawkins County, Tenn., only 17 percent of the families had not included pork in their diet during the week preceding the survey while 63 percent had eaten this type of meat every day. None of these families had had beef during the same week. At the opposite extreme in pork consumption was Washington County, Miss., in which 78 percent of the families had had no pork and an even larger proportion had been without beef. More than three-fifths of the families in the five counties, many of which contained children, had had no milk during the week prior to the survey and undoubtedly that week was not exceptional. Even those reporting milk did not always have it daily. The total lack of butter was even more frequent than the lack of milk, and little more than one-half of the families

---

[1] Moser, Ada M., *Farm Family Diets in the South Carolina Piedmont*, Circular 53, South Carolina Agricultural Experiment Station, Clemson, S. C., June 1935, p. 12.

[2] *Ibid.*, pp. 16–17.

[3] Phillips, Ark.; Concordia and Natchitoches, La.; Washington, Miss.; and Hawkins, Tenn.

[4] See, for example, White, H. C., "Dietary Studies in Georgia," *Dietary Studies in Rural Regions*, Bulletin 221, U. S. Department of Agriculture, Washington, D. C., 1909.

reported consuming eggs. Less than one out of five families had eggs daily, although it is usually possible for rural families to raise chickens. Families were also questioned concerning canned food on hand. Only one out of four had any canned goods available.[5] Yet the families were interviewed at some time between January and March 1939 when those who had canned food for winter consumption would still be expected to have a supply on hand. The five counties are admittedly not a representative sample of the Cotton South but it is believed that conditions are fairly typical of those among similar families throughout the region.[6]

Table 33.—Food Consumption of Low-Income Rural Families in 5 Southern Counties, January–March 1939

County and food item	Total families	Number of days families consumed specified food items during the week preceding the date of survey							
		None	1	2	3	4	5	6	7
PHILLIPS, ARK.									
Pork	115	84	5	3	6	3	1	1	12
Eggs	115	70	8	14	7	3	3	1	9
Milk	115	84	5	2	1	4	1	—	18
Butter	115	80	1	5	7	5	1	—	16
Beef	115	110	3	2	—	—	—	—	—
CONCORDIA, LA.									
Pork	167	116	16	14	6	3	1	—	11
Eggs	167	12	8	15	24	27	29	8	44
Milk	167	74	5	6	1	—	7	4	70
Butter	167	100	2	18	4	1	8	1	33
Beef	167	142	17	5	2	—	—	—	1
NATCHICTOHES, LA.									
Pork	170	107	9	8	5	2	1	—	38
Eggs	170	63	6	16	18	6	4	3	54
Milk	170	111	—	2	—	1	—	—	56
Butter	170	142	5	3	2	4	1	1	12
Beef	170	162	5	2	1	—	—	—	—
WASHINGTON, MISS.									
Pork	153	119	4	4	7	3	2	3	11
Eggs	153	121	9	13	3	—	1	2	4
Milk	153	118	9	8	5	—	1	2	10
Butter	153	130	6	4	2	1	1	4	5
Beef	153	143	7	2	—	—	—	1	—
HAWKINS, TENN.									
Pork	92	16	2	—	5	9	2	—	58
Eggs	92	57	4	4	6	4	—	—	17
Milk	92	49	3	1	1	4	—	—	34
Butter	92	39	8	4	5	3	1	1	31
Beef	92	92	—	—	—	—	—	—	—

Source: Survey of Rural Unemployed Not Receiving Public Aid, Division of Research, Works Progress Administration, Washington, D. C.

---

[5] Data on file, Division of Research, Work Projects Administration, Washington, D. C.

[6] See Dickens, Dorothy, *Family Living on Poorer and Better Soil*, Bulletin No. 320, Mississippi Agricultural Experiment Station, State College, Miss., September 1937, pp. 12–20.

Associated with the inadequacies of the diet of low-income farm families are the types of cooking that prevail. Hot breads, fried foods, and overcooked vegetables represent the common practices.[7]

In addition to the dietary value of production for home use, this type of agricultural enterprise is an important factor in raising the income level of the farm family. Sharecropper and share tenant families with the greatest production for home use tend to have the largest net incomes. Among 5,133 plantation families surveyed in 1934, it was found that the median net income for all families was $259 but for those families which had no production for home use the median was only $124.[8] The relation of such production to income is also indicated by a special analysis of croppers and share tenants on 89 Arkansas plantations. Food produced for home consumption amounted to 24 percent of the total net income of cropper families and 31 percent of the total for share tenant families.[9] Thus increased emphasis on gardens and livestock will not only improve diets and health but also will constitute one step toward raising the net incomes of poverty-stricken families.

HOUSING

The dietary inadequacies of the agricultural families at the bottom of the economic ladder in the Southern States are accompanied by poor housing. The observing traveler in the deep South is rudely shocked when he sees for the first time the widespread evidences of rural poverty revealed by farm homes. Houses, of poor construction to begin with, seldom are repaired either by the landlord or the occupant. Roofs and walls that need repairs, inadequate lighting, over-crowding, lack of other than primitive sanitary facilities, and bare yards edged by cotton fields are characteristic. A painted house is often indicative of considerable social as well as economic standing.

From a farm-housing survey made early in 1934, it is possible to derive a composite picture of farm housing in the South. The majority of Southern farm families do not own their homes. Most houses are old, and they are frequently in need of replacement or major repairs. In the South Atlantic and East South Central Divisions more than one-half of all farm houses were at least 25 years old at the time of the survey, and unpainted frame structures predominated. Houses are

---

[7] White, Max R., Ensminger, Douglas, and Gregory, Cecil L., *Rich Land—Poor People*, Research Report No. 1, U. S. Department of Agriculture, Farm Security Administration, Region III, Indianapolis, Ind., January 1938, p. 51.

[8] Woofter, T. J., Jr. and Others, *Landlord and Tenant on the Cotton Plantation*, Research Monograph V, Division of Social Research, Works Progress Administration, Washington, D. C., 1936, p. 221.

[9] Blalock, H. W., *Plantation Operations of Landlords and Tenants in Arkansas*, Bulletin No. 339, Arkansas Agricultural Experiment Station, Fayetteville, Ark., May 1937, p. 25.

Sharecropper Home.

usually of one story and contain four to five rooms. In neither the East South Central nor West South Central Division is there an average of even 1 closet per house and in the South Atlantic Division the average is only 1.1 closets. Bathrooms and basements are rarely found. While 23 percent of the farm houses in the South Atlantic Division had water supplied to the houses either by means of hand pumps in dwellings or piped from outside, this convenience was reported for only 9 percent of the farm homes in the East South Central Division and 17 percent in the West South Central Division. In all three divisions even fewer housewives had running water and the convenience of a kitchen sink with drain. Stoves or fireplaces in contrast to central heating systems are almost universally relied on for heat with wood the usual fuel for both heating and cooking. One measure of the widespread need for repairs is the fact that in all three Southern divisions one-third of the roofs, doors and windows, and interior walls and ceilings were reported to be in poor condition.[10] Because of such inadequacies Southern farm families are the most poorly housed farm families in any geographic region. Moreover, the averages are influenced by the more well-to-do farm families so that the above description represents better than average housing conditions among the cropper and laborer families.

Data from the recent Study of Consumer Purchases for white farm families in two counties in North Carolina and six counties in South Carolina, indicative of the general situation, show that lack of plumbing facilities is almost universal below the $1,000 income level (table 34). With more than 9 out of 10 households reporting no indoor water supply, the dangers from a health standpoint are obvious.

Table 34.—Plumbing Facilities Reported by White Farm Operator Families in 8 Counties [1] in North Carolina and South Carolina, by Income,[2] 1935–36

[Nonrelief families that include husband and wife, both native-born]

Income	Total families	Percent having specified facilities				
		Any indoor running water [3]	No indoor water supply	Running hot and cold water for bathtub or shower	Kitchen sink with drain	Indoor toilet
Less than $250	22	0.0	100.0	0.0	0.0	0.0
$250–$499	123	0.8	91.1	0.0	2.5	0.8
$500–$749	237	0.8	91.6	0.4	4.6	0.4
$750–$999	284	1.8	91.8	0.4	2.8	1.8

[1] Edgecome and Nash, N. C.; Clarendon, Darlington, Florence, Lee, Marion, and Sumter, S. C.
[2] Excludes families with incomes of $1,000 or more.
[3] Excludes indoor hand pumps, which were not classified as indoor running water.

Source: Study of Consumer Purchases, U. S. Department of Agriculture, Bureau of Home Economics, Washington, D. C., Preliminary release, June 15, 1938.

[10] Bureau of Home Economics, *The Farm-Housing Survey*, Miscellaneous Publication No. 323, U. S. Department of Agriculture, Washington, D. C., March 1939, *passim*.

HEALTH

By reason of the poor housing, inadequate sanitary facilities, unbalanced diets, and low educational level associated with their meager incomes, the poverty-stricken families in the rural South have high rates of illness which in turn constitute a tremendous drain on their slender resources. For example, well over one-half of the Southern farm families in the lowest income groups in 10 selected counties, families already certified as in need but not yet receiving public assistance, were in debt for medical care during January–March 1939.[11]

Not only do the ignorance and poverty of the Southern share-cropper and laborer operate against effective care of the sick but also the simple household equipment and sanitary facilities which are essential for the prevention of contagion are largely lacking among these groups. Moreover, public measures for control are less fully developed in rural than in urban areas. In a group of 40 Southern counties surveyed in 1936, two-thirds were found to lack adequate supervision to prevent the spread of the common childhood diseases of measles and whooping cough while one-third were below standard in the steps necessary for the control of scarlet fever.[12] As late as January 1939 six of the Southern States did not have State legislation making smallpox vaccination compulsory, and three additional States had only local option.

Three diseases which are readily controlled if proper preventive measures are applied and which remain major health problems in the rural South are typhoid and paratyphoid fever, pellagra, and malaria. That typhoid and paratyphoid fever can be brought under control with an effective program of prevention is illustrated by the decline in North Carolina from 35.8 deaths per 100,000 total population from this cause in 1914 to 2.3 deaths in 1937.[13] Some of the other Southern States have reduced the death rate from this cause to an even lower figure. Yet in 1936, 40 percent of all deaths from typhoid or paratyphoid fever in the United States occurred in the rural areas of 12 Southern States.[14]

Pellagra is much more prevalent in the South than records show; a large proportion of the persons affected never see a physician and the death rate is not a measure of incidence. The extent of the

[11] Data on file, Division of Research, Work Projects Administration, Washington, D. C.

[12] Technical Committee on Medical Care, *The Need for a National Health Program*, Interdepartmental Committee to Coordinate Health and Welfare Activities, Washington, D. C., 1938, p. 10.

[13] State Department of Health, Raleigh, N. C.

[14] Bureau of the Census, *Mortality Statistics: 1936*, U. S. Department of Commerce, Washington, D. C., 1938, table 5.

disease is in inverse correlation to family income. Since it is due to a faulty or unbalanced diet, a major step in its control within a given family is recognition of the need for cultivating a garden. This, however, is often difficult as the cotton sharecropper or tenant is ordinarily under pressure to devote his time and energies and acreage to the production of the money crop. Even when gardens are planted, the Southern agriculturist is prone to neglect winter vegetables and therefore has fresh vegetables for only part of the year. The importance of gardens is directly illustrated by the seasonal incidence of pellagra, which increases in the late winter or early spring after several months when fresh garden products are not generally available to low-income families. Because of the same circumstances, moreover, various other deficiency diseases, such as scurvy, beriberi, nutritional edema, and nutritional anemia, also occur throughout the South.[15]

That malaria is now primarily a Southern rural disease is indicated by the fact that rural areas of 12 Southern States accounted for more than two-thirds of all deaths from this cause in 1936.[16] Its toll is measured both by deaths and by morbidity rates. Such illness has been a serious factor in lowering the productivity of Southern workers. A tremendous advance in the control of malaria has been made in recent years, however, through the CWA, FERA, and WPA programs. Under these 3 programs almost 2,000,000 acres of swamps have been drained, affecting the health of 15,000,000 people.[17]

Another major health problem in the South is the control of venereal disease. Prevalence rates for syphilis have been found to be much higher among Negroes as a whole than among whites. Among both races, low incomes of rural families make public provision for treatment necessary.[18]

Associated with the inadequate control of various diseases are the insufficient provisions for infant and maternal care. The infant mortality rate (number of deaths under 1 year of age per 1,000 live births) in rural areas of the Eastern Old South region for 1930–1934 was 66 in comparison with a rate of 57 for the United States.[19] In the three Southern geographic divisions combined the rural infant mortality rate for 1933–1935 was 56 per 1,000 for white infants and 80 per 1,000

[15] Sebrell, W. H., "The Nature of Nutritional Diseases Occurring in the South," *The Milbank Memorial Fund Quarterly*, October 1939, pp. 358–366.

[16] Bureau of the Census, *Mortality Statistics: 1936, op. cit.*

[17] Works Progress Administration, *Inventory*, Washington, D. C., 1938, p. 44.

[18] Clark, Taliaferro, *The Control of Syphilis in Southern Rural Areas*, Julius Rosenwald Fund, Chicago, Ill., 1932, pp. 5–6; and Burney, L. E., "Control of Syphilis in a Southern Rural Area," *American Journal of Public Health*, September 1939, pp. 1006–1014.

[19] Mangus, A. R., *Rural Regions of the United States*, Division of Research, Work Projects Administration, Washington, D. C., 1940, table 5.

for Negro infants.[20]   A physician was in attendance at only one out of
five Negro births in rural districts in 1935, and practically none of the
births occurred in hospitals.[21]   This dependence upon midwives
rather than physicians at birth is widespread among the poorer white
families as well as among Negro families.   In a survey of 16 rural
counties in Georgia during the winter of 1935–36, it was found that
of 770 confinements among white women 14 per cent were attended
by midwives; of 650 confinements among Negro women 82.9 percent
were attended by midwives.[22]

A further index of the inadequacy of health services is the limited
hospital facilities.   In the Georgia survey referred to above it was
found that 9 of the 16 counties had some hospital facilities but only
2 of the 9 had an adequate number of beds.   Moreover, most of the
counties had no public provision for the care of the indigent sick.
Such data are illustrative of conditions not only in the limited area
surveyed but also throughout much of the rural South.   Even where
hospital facilities have been provided, the isolated farm family may
be cut off from such benefits by transportation difficulties.

One of the most effective methods of meeting the medical needs of
low-income farm families is through county plans for medical care
developed by the Farm Security Administration in cooperation with
State medical associations.[23]   By January 1939 such programs had
been put into operation in 59 Arkansas counties, in 12 Mississippi
counties, and less widely in Alabama, Georgia, Oklahoma, Tennessee,
and Texas.   Plans are also under way for extension of the program
into several other Southern States.

Much emphasis has been placed on the importance of the educational training received by Southern rural children to other sections
of the country to which many of them will migrate.   It is also germane
to emphasize their physical well-being.   If they are subject to various
chronic diseases or have uncorrected disabilities, they may be dan-
gerous to others or less effectual producers themselves.   Thus,
improved health facilities for the South will have an economic value
not only for the section itself but also for the other sections which
draw upon its surplus population.

[20] Tandy, Elizabeth C., *Infant and Maternal Mortality Among Negroes*, Bureau
Publication No. 243, U. S. Department of Labor, Children's Bureau, Washington,
D. C., 1937, p. 12.

[21] *Ibid.*, p. 7.

[22] Conducted by the Medical Association of Georgia and the State Department
of Health with the cooperation of the United States Public Health Service.   See
Proceedings of the National Health Conference, Washington, D. C., July 18, 19, 20,
1938, pp. 81–82.

[23] Williams, R. C., "Medical Care Plans for Low-Income Farm Families,"
The Health Officer, Vol. 3, January 1939, pp. 245–252.

EDUCATION

Dire poverty and lack of education constitute one of the many vicious circles which characterize large areas of the rural South. Comparisons of expenditures per child, teachers' salaries, length of school term, and related items for the Southern States and all other States need not be repeated here.[24] By every educational criterion Southern States as a group rank lowest in spite of the very appreciable advances in educational facilities which have occurred within the last few years. In any effort to farm intelligently, to spend his limited income to the best advantage, to raise his status either economically or socially, the average Southern farm dweller faces the handicap of inadequate education. Not only is this true of the older generation but even more serious is the fact that the rising generation is also lagging well below the educational average for the country as a whole.

Most of the Southern States make strenuous efforts to support their schools but limited financial resources plus high fertility rates and the necessity of supporting two separate school systems, one for white children and one for Negro children, make the provision of opportunities commensurate with those in the wealthier States impossible. The Southeastern farm population, which received only 2.2 percent of the national income in 1930, was faced with the responsibility of educating 13.4 percent of all children of school age. For the entire South the proportion of the national income received by the farm population was 3.4 percent, but the proportion of the Nation's children of school age was 17.2 percent.[25]

In the face of lack of information on the educational attainments of the general population, the extent of illiteracy in the South has been particularly stressed. An effective attack on this problem has been made through the Emergency Education Program of the FERA–WPA under which, from 1933 through June 1938, more than one-half million persons in both urban and rural areas of 12 Southern States [26] were taught to read and write. These States accounted for more than 50 percent of all persons in the United States who achieved literacy as a result of the program. While learning to read and write may be accomplished without the individual becoming functionally literate, it is an important first step, and its attainment by such numbers

[24] For data see Office of Education, *Biennial Survey of Education in the United States*, U. S. Department of the Interior, Washington, D. C.; Woofter, T. J., Jr. and Others, *Landlord and Tenant on the Cotton Plantation*, Research Monograph V, Division of Social Research, Works Progress Administration, Washington, D. C., 1936, ch. IX; and Edwards, Newton, *Equal Educational Opportunity for Youth*, American Council on Education, Washington, D. C., 1939.

[25] Edwards, Newton, *op. cit.*, p. 88.

[26] Alabama, Arkansas, Georgia, Kentucky, Louisiana, Mississippi, North Carolina, Oklahoma, South Carolina, Tennessee, Texas, and Virginia.

represents a tremendous achievement. Since there were more than 2 million illiterates in the 12 States in 1930, however, there are far greater numbers still to be taught if illiteracy rates are to drop to a minimum. While adult education can hardly be overemphasized, the major stress must be upon the rising generation. The public schools must increase their effectiveness in Southern rural areas if all children capable of learning to read and write are to become truly literate. Unless this is done the Southern States will continue to have a sizable group which is ill-equipped to manage its own affairs.

That the extent of illiteracy increases as one descends the economic scale is well known. The relationship between these two factors among Negro agricultural workers has been summarized as follows: "* * * there is a much greater tendency for Negroes to be able to read and write when they independently operate small farms for themselves, or if a family or so of them work for a single white family, than there is if they are grouped together in large numbers as wage hands, croppers, or share tenants on the plantations." [27]

One recently available source of information on educational attainment is the data for relief households. These materials are indicative of the educational status of a much larger proportion of the population than that actually on relief because in the South the number of destitute families has far exceeded the capacities of the relief program. [28] In a survey of heads of open country households on relief in October 1935 it was found that 1 out of 10 white heads and 3 out of 10 Negro heads in the Eastern Cotton Area had had no formal schooling (table 35). Less than 1 in 4 of the white heads and only 1 in 25 of the Negro heads had advanced beyond the seventh grade. Moreover, the children in relief households had a poor attendance record with one out of nine of the white children and about one out of five of the Negro children, even within the compulsory attendance ages of 7–13 years, not attending school (table 36).

In October, the survey month, cotton picking is a factor in poor school attendance, because in the Southeast the children of the household are expected to join their elders in the fields whenever requirements for hand labor mount. Cotton picking may extend throughout the autumn months and may keep children out of school until January unless the school is adjusted to the cotton cycle. Labor needs during the planting season also interrupt school attendance for many children. Tobacco likewise utilizes much child labor in Southeastern farming areas, and hours are long.

[27] Smith, T. Lynn, *The Population of Louisiana: Its Composition and Changes*, Louisiana Bulletin No. 293, Louisiana State University, Baton Rouge, La., November 1937, p. 67.

[28] See ch. VI.

Table 35.—School Attainment of Heads of Open Country Families in the Eastern Cotton Area Receiving General Relief, by Color, October 1935

Last grade or year completed	Total	White	Negro
Total	2,946	2,300	646
	Percent distribution		
Total	100.0	100.0	100.0
Grade and high school:			
None	14.5	10.3	29.7
1–3	21.2	17.6	34.1
4–7	45.7	49.6	32.2
8	8.8	10.6	1.9
9–11	7.6	9.3	1.5
12	0.6	0.8	—
College:			
1–3	0.9	1.1	—
4 or more	0.7	0.7	0.6

Source: Zimmerman, Carle C., and Whetten, Nathan L., *Rural Families on Relief*, Research Monograph XVII, Division of Social Research, Works Progress Administration, Washington, D. C., 1938, p. 147.

Table 36.—Percent of the Open Country General Relief Population 7 Through 17 Years of Age in the Eastern Cotton Area Attending School, by Color, October 1935

Age	Percent attending school		
	Total	White	Negro
7–13 years	87.4	89.1	81.9
14–15 years	72.0	73.9	65.3
16–17 years	26.1	29.8	13.8

Source: Mangus, A. R., *Changing Aspects of Rural Relief*, Research Monograph XIV, Division of Social Research, Works Progress Administration, Washington, D. C., 1938, p. 154.

In addition to the demand for their labor, the children in many farm sections of the South still face such handicaps in attaining an education as inaccessibility of schools, health problems, lack of books, and lack of clothes (appendix table 25). Except in States providing transportation to consolidated schools, dirt roads and long distances form a combination that makes school attendance virtually impossible for many children, both white and Negro, except under the most favorable weather conditions. There is a direct relationship, moreover, between retardation, as measured by the percent of children who are over-age for their grades, and distance from school (table 37). The farther the child has to go to attend school the less likely he is to make normal progress. The indifference of many parents, themselves illiterate or only semi-literate, is another factor that weighs heavily both in nonattendance and in irregular attendance. Among those segments of the Southern rural population which are least educated themselves, the attainment of even an elementary school education by their children is least valued.

Table 37.—Negro Rural Children Who Are Over-age for Their Grade, by Distance to School [1]

Distance to school	Percent over-age
Less than 1 mile	65.1
1–1½ miles	71.5
2–2½ miles	75.1
3–3½ miles	76.9
4–4½ miles	77.5
5 miles or more	79.2

[1] Based on a study of 638 rural schools in 28 counties of 6 Southern States.

Source: Caliver, Ambrose, *Availability of Education to Negroes in Rural Communities*, Bulletin, 1935, No. 12, U. S. Department of the Interior, Office of Education, Washington, D. C., 1936, p. 66.

Though the general trend throughout the United States to raise the age limits for compulsory school attendance is also in operation in the South, the only States which still have minimum age requirements as low as 14 and 15 years are found in that section. Whatever the age limits, laxity in enforcement may more or less nullify the effects.

Another marked trend affecting rural education is the abandonment of one-room schools, but two-room schools are still widespread. According to a recent review by the United States Office of Education, Texas has nearly 3,000 two-room schools, Tennessee nearly 2,000 two-room schools, and most other Southern States approximately 1,000 such schools.[29]

Concomitant with the disappearance of the smallest rural units is the trend toward consolidation and the increase in high school facilities. Most rural schools in the South, however, cannot compete with large urban schools in the variety of training offered to students. Training at the high school level is usually traditional in character with the exception of agricultural and home economics courses and possibly elementary commercial work. Although commendable in themselves, they are not sufficient to meet the increasingly apparent need for vocational education and guidance.

While there is definite need for the expansion of high school opportunities, this should not overshadow the fact that among the lowest income groups the emphasis must for the present remain on the elementary school. In a recent Julius Rosenwald Fund report, the basic program needed by elementary rural schools in the South was summarized as follows:

"The first and great reform in rural schools * * * is that education shall direct itself to the peculiar needs of country children with a view to making them happy and useful citizens of country life.

[29] Cook, Katherine M., "Review of Conditions and Developments in Education in Rural and Other Sparsely Settled Areas," *Biennial Survey of Education in the United States: 1934–36*, U. S. Department of the Interior, Office of Education, Washington, D. C., 1937, Vol. I, ch. V, pp. 3–4.

Let us look for a moment at the kind of preparation children need for rural living. Five items stand out—(1) the ability to read (and write) clearly and understandingly; (2) some skill in the use of figures; (3) knowledge of farming, including some general understanding of biological processes and an appreciation of nature; (4) manual dexterity, especially in the handling of wood, fabrics, and other materials, and in simple mechanics; (5) health. These are self-evident necessities for any successful life in the country. It seems naive to argue the need of education in such obvious items. But the simple fact is that rural children are not getting from their schools anything approaching adequate preparation in these fundamentals. * * *

"These five subjects we submit as the essentials of the elementary school in a rural district. If children gain competence in these, they may live happily and successfully. Surely the learning of five broad topics is not too much to expect from the 6 to 8 years of the common school."[30]

Regardless of the extent of opportunities beyond the elementary school, the achievement of this basic education by every open country child, white and Negro, in the South would represent a fundamental step in raising not only the educational level but also the general social and economic level.

PLANE OF LIVING

The low level of living and restricted opportunities of the average farm family in the South are emphasized by the rural-farm plane-of-living index (fig. 11). This index combines the average value of the

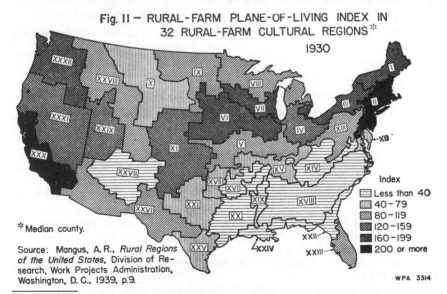

Fig. 11 — RURAL-FARM PLANE-OF-LIVING INDEX IN 32 RURAL-FARM CULTURAL REGIONS *

1930

Index
☐ Less than 40
▥ 40-79
▨ 80-119
▦ 120-159
▩ 160-199
■ 200 or more

*Median county.

Source: Mangus, A. R., *Rural Regions of the United States*, Division of Research, Work Projects Administration, Washington, D. C., 1939, p. 9.

WPA 3314

[30] Embree, Edwin R., *Julius Rosenwald Fund*, Review for the Two-Year Period 1933–35, Chicago, Ill., 1935, pp. 5 and 10.

farm dwelling, the percent of farms having automobiles, the percent of farm homes having electric lights, the percent having running water piped into the house, the percent having telephones, and the percent having radios in 1930.[31]   On this basis the rural-farm indices for the Eastern Old South, Mississippi Delta, and Western Old South Regions were 26, 16, and 26, respectively, in comparison with the United States average of 100.   These three regions, practically coterminous with the Cotton South, have the lowest indices of any region except the Ozark-Ouachita Region.[32]   Moreover, while these areas have high proportions of Negroes, a low level of living is characteristic of white tenants and laborers as well as Negroes, as previous sections of this analysis have indicated.

One of the most promising developments for improving general living conditions in the South is the expansion of electrical service.   Great strides have been made in this direction in several Southern States within the last 4 years, but not one of them is yet up to the national average of 22.1 percent of all farms receiving central-station service, June 30, 1939 [33] (table 38).   The importance of electricity in raising the standard of living does not stop with lights and such electrical equipment as can be afforded but it also facilitates the use of pressure water systems for household plumbing.[34] This in turn carries important health benefits as it means a protected water supply.

Table 38.—Farms in 12 Southern States Receiving Central-Station Service, June 30, 1939

State	Estimated number of farms receiving service	Percent of estimated number of farms in State [1]
Alabama	27, 500	9. 6
Arkansas	8, 000	3. 2
Georgia	34, 965	13. 7
Kentucky	22, 789	7. 7
Louisiana	12, 474	7. 2
Mississippi	11, 641	3. 6
North Carolina	59, 580	18. 6
Oklahoma	9, 968	4. 8
South Carolina	22, 562	14. 7
Tennessee	29, 000	10. 1
Texas	44, 484	9. 3
Virginia	40, 893	20. 5

[1] United States percent=22.1.

Source: Unpublished data, Rural Electrification Administration, Washington, D. C., October 24, 1939.

[31] Lively, C. E. and Almack, R. B., *A Method of Determining Rural Social Sub-Areas With Application to Ohio*, Mimeograph Bulletin No. 106, Ohio State University and Ohio Agricultural Experiment Station, Columbus, Ohio, January 1938.

[32] Mangus, A. R., *op. cit.*, p. 37.

[33] Unpublished data, Rural Electrification Administration, Washington, D. C., October 14, 1939.

[34] *Report of the Rural Electrification Administration: 1938*, Washington, D. C., January 1939, p. 24.

While the advantages are obvious, the poverty of many Southern farmers is such that they cannot meet the costs incident even to the most economical program for providing electricity. Those farmers who have this facility are the more well-to-do operators and the possibilities of electricity becoming available to the average sharecropper or farm laborer, let alone his being able to purchase appliances, appear to be slight under present conditions.

Directly related to plane of living as well as to education is the availability of reading materials. Here, too, most Southern States lag, with restricted public library facilities and with limited circulation of magazines (appendix tables 26 and 27). Virginia is the only one of the 12 Southern States analyzed which approaches the United States average in volumes per capita in public libraries. North Carolina, which leads the group of States in the proportion of the rural population residing in local public library districts, had only 30.3 percent of the rural population in such districts in 1934. At the opposite extreme was Arkansas with only 2.9 percent. Circulation of magazines is primarily dependent upon the economic and educational level of individual families. So far as 47 national magazines are concerned the 12 Southern States studied rank at the bottom among the 48 States. They make a somewhat better showing on circulation of farm publications with four States above the national average.

The problems of rural living in the South described in terms of need for balanced diets, improved housing, control of disease, better schools, and availability of such items as radios and magazines all reflect the economic situation. There are also the related questions of lives characterized by drudgery and monotony and of the need for changing attitudes and habits and broadening cultural horizons. The cotton cycle is such that periods of heavy labor demands are interspersed with long periods when little time is required for farm operations. In general the low-income Southern farm family lacks the training, the facilities, and the incentive to take advantage of these periods of leisure either for improving its surroundings or for self-improvement. The need for broad programs for social and economic reconstruction should not obscure the possibilities of helping the individual family to improve its own living conditions.

Chapter VIII

PROGRAMS AND POLICIES

A COMMISSION appointed by President Roosevelt in 1937 to report on conditions in the South characterized the region as economic problem number one. From the foregoing pages the rural aspects of this problem take on definite form.

During the 1930's Southern farm families have added approximately two and a half million potential workers to the labor supply. The recent industrial expansion has absorbed only a fraction of this number, resulting in tremendous pressure of population on the economic resources of the region.

Demand for the products of agriculture has been drastically reduced by the loss of foreign markets and by the shrinkage in purchasing power of the unemployed group. Meanwhile, mechanization and improved practices have actually reduced the number of families required by the plantation economy. Owner cash incomes have improved in the late 1930's, and this class has increased its investment and reduced its debt. But incomes for plantation croppers and share tenants in the year of exceptionally large production, 1937, while above the 1934 level, averaged only about $400, including production for home use. In the years 1938 and 1939, when the total value of the cotton crop was reduced by a third under that of 1937, a drastic decline both in tenant income and in the extent of employment of seasonal labor resulted.

Thus, neither industry nor agriculture has absorbed the excess new workers. Displacement from agriculture has actually added to the total of idle workers, and a large proportion of the tenants do not make enough to live on through the winter. This low-income agricultural group has added tremendously to the task of the agencies of relief and reconstruction.

71

The plantation study made in 1934 [1] concluded with a series of recommendations. The principal proposals may be listed as follows:

1. Retirement of submarginal lands from agriculture.

2. Improvement of conservation practices on lands remaining in agriculture, including erosion control and reforestation.

3. Promotion of family-sized, owner-operated farms to balance the commercial plantation system and absorb more of the displaced agricultural population.

4. Reinforcement of the family-sized farm by the development of cooperative devices.

5. Promotion of diversified farming.

6. Coordination of production control and soil conservation.

7. Credit reform.

8. Tenancy reform in the direction of (1) promoting ownership and (2) improving the status of tenants and protecting their security through State legislation and written leases.

9. Continuation and expansion of the Federal work program to care for a larger proportion of the families in need.

10. Continuation and expansion of the rehabilitation program to aid an increasing number of low-income farmers to establish their farm operations on a sound basis.

11. Equalization of the social services, especially in health and education, by use of the broader base of taxation of the Federal Government.

To these should be added:

12. Adaptation of housing programs for low-income groups to Southern rural conditions.

Social change is inevitably a slow process and these objectives can not be accomplished overnight. It is appropriate, however, to check on the extent of the accomplishment of these aims since 1934.

1. Submarginal land retirement designed to take lands of low fertility out of agriculture has proceeded slowly under small appropriations. The original appropriations have provided for the purchase of 9 million acres of land, and the program is now operated in connection with the Soil Conservation Service.

2. Soil conservation has been vigorously promoted and more progress made in the 1930's than in the previous 100 years. Experimentation and demonstration of improved practices have developed rapidly, and many States have passed acts authorizing the formation of soil conservation districts within which the farmers can democratically determine the use of the land and receive aid from the Soil

---

[1] See Woofter, T. J., Jr. and Others, *Landlord and Tenant on the Cotton Plantation*, Research Monograph V, Division of Social Research, Works Progress Administration, Washington, D. C., 1936.

Conservation Service in inaugurating improved practices. The number of districts so authorized in the South is 73 or nearly half of the total in the United States.

Reforestation contributes not only to the rebuilding of exhausted soil but also to the preservation of valuable natural resources. A large proportion of the submarginal lands purchased has been included in national and State forests. Any program for rehabilitation in the South must take into account the fact that 30 percent of Southern lands are in forests. The infant pulp industry in the South can probably develop a market for slash pine as a money crop, but even the fast-growing slash pine takes a number of years to mature and the investment over these years requires more capital than low-income farmers have available.

3. The promotion of family-sized farms has not been attacked directly except in the case of the rehabilitation borrowers and tenant purchase clients of the Farm Security Administration. Well over 300,000 of these, chosen from the lowest income group in the South, have been placed on family-sized farms and started on the road to ownership. They have undergone marked improvement in financial position and level of living through careful planning of their operations. The average net worth of 116,000 Southern families included in a survey made as of the end of the 1938 crop year had increased from $451 to $752 since they had been under the guidance of the rehabilitation program.

The readjustment of the land to the population is necessarily a slow development and requires considerable aid to individual initiative. Available tracts are often too large or require too much capital outlay for drainage or improvement to adapt them to small holdings. Government purchase of such lands for resale after improvement would facilitate the increase of small holdings and the accommodation of more people on the land.

4. The promotion of cooperation among small holders has been approached experimentally by the Farm Security Administration. The size of cooperative enterprises varies greatly. Some farms have been set up on a completely cooperative basis, some with individual operating units and cooperative ownership of stores, gins, and heavy machinery, and some with cooperation among a few farmers in the ownership of a registered sire or a piece of heavy machinery. The real task of promoting cooperation is, however, one of education and will be a long process.

5. Diversification is making progress in the South as is indicated by estimated increases in the proportion of the cash income from livestock and by the ratio of home-use production to cash income. The full development of a balanced general farm program is retarded, however, by the lack of large urban markets.

6. The more recent conservation legislation and programs of the Department of Agriculture have emphasized benefits paid for the cultivation of soil-conserving crops planted on acreage formerly devoted to staple crops. This has had the double objective of controlling the supply of agricultural products with a resulting stabilization of prices and at the same time conserving the soil. The one year in which cotton production was relatively uncontrolled and the one year in which tobacco restrictions were removed were sufficient to pile up surpluses in these commodities which, were well-nigh ruinous to the producers. There seems to be no immediate hope of recovery of a sufficient foreign market to restore cotton to its former export position unless prices are drastically lowered. Also, the outlook for tobacco exports is not promising in view of the current European situation. A program of control is, therefore, basic to the welfare of the cotton and tobacco farmers.

7. Credit reform has aided the owner operators but has not extended to the tenants. The owner's average rate of interest on mortgages has been reduced by shifting mortgage debts from private to governmental agencies. There has, however, been only slight improvement in the production credit situation for either the owner or the tenant.

8. Commendable beginnings have been made in attacking the problem of tenancy. The Bankhead-Jones bill provides a small sum for financing tenants who wish to become owners and allows them a long period for repayment. Of necessity, this program had to be small in the beginning, and up to July 1939 the Farm Security Administration had approved only about 3,200 tenant purchase loans in 14 Southern States. If the land and the funds were available, thousands of other tenants could be started on the road to ownership. These farms are practical units from the viewpoint of the ability of the land to produce the purchase price over a period of years. Every effort is made to improve the land and buildings insofar as is consistent with economy. The result in many areas is a homestead which stands out as a bright example in the midst of surrounding unimproved tenant farms. Thus, while the quality of these farms is a distinct advance, their quantity is far below the existing need.

In improvement of leases, progress has been made with those farmers who were so low in the economic scale as to become eligible for Farm Security Administration loans; some 72,000 of them have written leases. The movement for State legislation requiring such leases is just beginning, however.

9. The Federal work program provides employment for several hundred thousand rural families. As long as population increases and labor displacements are not absorbed by industry or agriculture, a program of public employment will be necessary. The present operation of the program is hampered in rural areas by the lack of

construction skills by the workers involved and the poverty of sponsoring communities. For this reason the rural program should tend more and more in the direction of providing rural services, such as education, sanitation, recreational facilities, and electrification, and necessary work in reforestation and soil conservation. The Work Projects Administration has not in the past conducted projects of all these types. Modifications in the 1941 act with reference to such work should provide for increased employment along these lines and should greatly facilitate the programs of forest and erosion control and rural electrification. As indicated in the discussion of relief needs, the funds available for the work programs in the South have never been sufficient to care for the large number of needy families.

10. The rehabilitation program of the Farm Security Administration has been expanded since its inception in 1934 until nearly 350,000 farmers in the South have been aided with loans and 150,000 with emergency grants. Of these, nearly 250,000 remained active loan cases in the summer of 1939 in the sense that they were securing advice and supervision in their farming and homemaking problems. This service is as important as, if not more important than, the financial aid offered to these low-income farmers whose rehabilitation is usually as much a task of education and supervision as it is of financial aid. Here also funds have been inadequate for the magnitude of the task, and the difficulties are complicated by the increasing scarcity in some counties of available good land for rehabilitation clients.

11. Federal assistance for rural sections which are financially unable to attain urban standards for social services in spite of heavy tax burdens has been strongly advocated by three recent Presidential committees or conferences—one in the field of education, one in public health, and one in child welfare.

These groups have emphasized the fact that the future of the Nation is largely dependent on the care and rearing of the children in low-income families since these families include by far the largest number of children and are largely located in the areas of the most inadequate institutions. The children from these families enter the labor market in all sections of the country. Legislation looking toward the equalization of opportunity in education, public health, and child welfare by Federal grants based on need has been strongly recommended, but as yet no action has been taken.

12. The program of lending for the improvement and construction of owned houses as operated by the Federal Housing Authority is, of course, available to urban and rural dwellers alike. A vigorous program for low-income housing, such as that operated by the United

States Housing Authority, could provide not only improved living conditions but also much nonfarm employment for the rural population. Considerable progress has been made in the development of programs for urban housing, but despite the urgent need the adaptation of these programs to rural conditions has lagged far behind. Without some such subsidy as that included in the urban housing projects, it will be nearly impossible to build adequate rural houses which can be paid for out of the income from the land.

Although marked progress has been made in meeting certain problems and little in meeting others, the numerous books, reports, and discussions of the past few years dealing with conditions in the South have stimulated public opinion to such an extent that it is far more enlightened and unified than ever before with respect to Southern needs. While the report of the President's Committee on Economic Conditions in the South [2] was factual and contained no recommendations, the public discussion which followed in Southern communities and organizations resulted in substantial agreement on the recommendations outlined above, adding, on the nonagricultural side, the need for extension of industrial development, tariff reform, and adjustment of inequities in freight rates. With substantial agreement of enlightened opinion as to the things which need to be done, it should be safe to predict that over a period of time major achievements will result.

[2] National Emergency Council, *Report on Economic Conditions of the South*, Washington, D. C., 1938.

Appendixes

Appendices

Appendix A

SUPPLEMENTARY TABLES

Table 1.—Crop Acres per Plantation, by Area, 1934–1938

Area	Total planta-tions	Crop acres per plantation				
		1938	1937	1936	1935	1934
All areas	246	473	477	460	397	417
Atlantic Coast Plain	31	321	331	322	233	243
Black Belt (A)	31	354	350	342	282	303
Black Belt (B)	16	237	243	247	250	249
Upper Delta	79	574	579	546	491	542
Lower Delta	19	364	373	375	256	249
Interior Plain	17	396	397	382	370	340
Mississippi Bluffs	27	438	434	420	399	392
Red River	15	711	718	706	557	535
Arkansas River	11	934	940	900	778	880

Table 2.—Crop Acres on Plantations, by Area, 1937 and 1934

Area	Total planta-tions	Number of plantations with specified acres in crops												
		Less than 200 acres		200–399 acres		400–599 acres		600–799 acres		800–999 acres		1,000–1,199 acres		1,200 acres or more	
		1937	1934	1937	1934	1937	1934	1937	1934	1937	1934	1937	1934	1937	1934
All areas	246	59	71	82	87	34	38	33	16	15	17	12	9	11	8
Atlantic Coast Plain	31	9	15	15	13	2	2	3	1	2	—	—	—	—	—
Black Belt (A)	31	12	10	10	14	3	5	4	1	1	1	1	—	—	—
Black Belt (B)	16	6	5	8	9	2	2	—	—	—	—	—	—	—	—
Upper Delta	79	10	14	25	24	12	14	18	6	5	11	4	7	5	3
Lower Delta	19	6	10	6	7	3	—	2	1	1	1	—	—	1	—
Interior Plain	17	4	5	7	7	2	4	2	—	1	—	1	1	—	—
Mississippi Bluffs	27	10	10	6	6	4	4	2	4	2	1	3	1	—	1
Red River	15	1	1	4	6	4	3	—	2	2	2	2	—	2	1
Arkansas River	11	1	1	1	1	2	4	2	1	1	1	1	—	3	3

Table 3.—Organization of Cropland per Plantation,[1] by Area, 1937 and 1934

Item	All areas		Atlantic Coast Plain		Black Belt (A)		Black Belt (B)		Upper Delta		Lower Delta		Interior Plain		Mississippi Bluffs		Red River		Arkansas River	
	1937	1934	1937	1934	1937	1934	1937	1934	1937	1934	1937	1934	1937	1934	1937	1934	1937	1934	1937	1934
Total plantations	246		31		31		16		79		19		17		27		15		11	
Crop acres per plantation																				
All crops	464	400	318	230	341	296	198	197	572	533	303	194	397	340	434	358	718	535	940	879
Cotton	230	178	99	70	100	80	74	66	323	243	144	97	179	146	210	173	408	285	527	521
Corn and interplanted legumes	134	148	126	98	150	137	73	78	142	200	69	81	155	139	148	148	182	144	127	195
Small grain[2]	18	13	25	11	25	20	25	32	13	9	7	3	15	11	6	2	6	12	94	40
Cowpea and soybean hay	20	14	12	5	8	6	9	12	22	24	9	3	1	17	32	12	17	8	84	20
Alfalfa hay	12	9	—	—	3	1	—	—	28	21	14	—	—	*	1	1	16	26	20	7
Other hay crops	9	9	2	2	3	3	5	3	6	8	37	—	7	2	9	3	12	40	24	72
Cowpeas and soybeans for seed	3	1	4	1	1	1	1	1	2	1	1	2	2	—	*	2	20	*	4	7
Truck, garden, and orchard	12	10	11	8	11	9	9	4	19	13	4	6	10	23	8	10	4	3	17	5
All other crops[3]	26	18	39	35	41	39	2	1	17	14	18	2	28	2	20	7	53	17	43	12
Percent distribution																				
All crops	100.0	100.0	100.0	100.0	100.0	100.0	100.0	100.0	100.0	100.0	100.0	100.0	100.0	100.0	100.0	100.0	100.0	100.0	100.0	100.0
Cotton	49.6	44.5	31.1	30.4	29.3	27.0	37.5	33.5	56.6	45.7	47.6	50.1	45.0	42.9	48.4	48.2	56.8	53.2	56.1	59.1
Corn and interplanted legumes	28.9	37.0	39.5	42.6	44.1	46.4	36.9	39.7	24.8	37.5	22.8	41.8	39.0	40.9	34.1	41.3	25.3	26.9	13.5	22.2
Small grain[2]	3.9	3.3	7.9	4.8	7.3	6.8	12.6	16.2	2.3	1.7	2.3	1.5	3.8	3.2	1.4	0.6	0.8	2.2	10.0	4.6
Cowpea and soybean hay	4.3	3.5	3.8	2.2	2.3	2.0	4.5	6.1	3.8	4.5	3.0	1.5	0.3	5.0	7.4	3.4	2.4	1.5	8.9	2.3
Alfalfa hay	2.6	2.2	—	—	0.9	0.3	—	—	4.9	3.9	4.6	—	—	*	0.2	0.3	2.2	4.9	2.1	0.8
Other hay crops	1.9	2.2	0.6	0.9	0.9	0.9	2.5	1.5	1.0	1.5	12.2	—	1.8	0.6	2.1	0.8	1.7	7.5	2.6	8.2
Cowpeas and soybeans for seed	0.6	0.3	1.3	0.4	0.3	0.3	0.5	0.5	0.3	0.2	0.3	1.0	0.5	—	*	0.6	2.8	*	0.4	0.8
Truck, garden, and orchard	2.6	2.5	3.5	3.5	3.2	3.0	4.5	2.0	3.3	2.4	1.3	3.1	2.5	6.8	1.8	2.8	0.6	0.6	1.8	0.6
All other crops[3]	5.6	4.5	12.3	15.2	12.0	13.2	1.0	0.5	3.0	2.6	5.9	1.0	7.1	0.6	4.6	2.0	7.4	3.2	4.6	1.4

* Less than 0.5 acre or 0.05 percent.

[1] Excludes cropland of renters (cash and standing) for which data by crops were not available.
[2] Principally oats.
[3] In the Atlantic Coast Plain and Black Belt (A) Areas approximately 10 percent of the crop acres were devoted to tobacco and/or peanuts.

Table 4.—Cotton Acreage on Plantations, by Area, 1937 and 1934

Area	Total planta- tions	Number of plantations with specified percent of crop acres in cotton															
		Less than 20 percent		20–29 percent		30–39 percent		40–49 percent		50–59 percent		60–69 percent		70–79 percent		80 percent or more	
		1937	1934	1937	1934	1937	1934	1937	1934	1937	1934	1937	1934	1937	1934	1937	1934
All areas	1 246	14	15	27	38	53	55	46	59	53	46	37	14	11	10	5	5
Atlantic Coast Plain	31	6	5	9	12	9	10	6	1	1	2	—	1	—	—	—	—
Black Belt (A)	31	6	7	7	12	13	10	4	2	—	—	1	—	—	—	—	—
Black Belt (B)	16	—	—	3	6	6	5	5	4	2	1	—	—	—	—	—	—
Upper Delta	79	—	1	—	—	6	17	13	27	21	24	28	4	7	5	4	1
Lower Delta	19	2	1	4	1	3	2	4	6	2	2	1	1	2	2	1	—
Interior Plain	17	—	—	—	—	5	4	6	5	3	6	1	1	—	—	—	—
Mississippi Bluffs	27	—	1	2	4	7	5	4	7	12	3	2	3	—	2	—	2
Red River	15	—	—	—	2	4	2	2	3	6	5	1	1	2	—	—	2
Arkansas River	11	—	—	—	—	—	—	2	4	6	3	3	3	—	1	—	—

1 In 1934, 4 plantations in the Lower Delta Area were rented out and cotton acreage was not available.

Table 5.—Yield of Lint Cotton per Acre, by Type of Tenants and Area, 1937 and 1934

Area	Total plantations		Yield of lint cotton per acre (pounds)							
			Total		Wage laborers		Croppers		Share tenants	
	1937	1934	1937	1934	1937	1934	1937	1934	1937	1934
All areas	1 244	2 242	456	268	445	278	468	263	432	274
Atlantic Coast Plain	31	31	322	277	326	269	332	283	264	259
Black Belt (A)	31	31	292	255	329	276	275	257	453	170
Black Belt (B)	16	16	323	305	359	338	303	288	425	305
Upper Delta	79	79	550	303	562	274	556	307	508	310
Lower Delta	17	15	452	253	554	299	484	228	273	253
Interior Plain	17	17	265	192	217	209	283	183	332	214
Mississippi Bluffs	27	27	504	278	543	249	503	288	464	251
Red River	15	15	392	247	388	280	405	223	193	212
Arkansas River	11	11	356	188	341	287	396	172	259	147

1 2 plantations in the Lower Delta Area reported no cotton produced by the specified types of tenants.
3 4 plantations in the Lower Delta Area reported no cotton produced by the specified types of tenants.

Table 6.—Resident Families 1 on Plantations, by Area and Type, 1934–1938

Area and type of family	1938	1937	1936	1935	1934
ALL AREAS					
Total	4, 058	4, 020	3, 943	3, 788	3, 738
Wage laborer	674	618	568	531	534
Cropper	2, 600	2, 598	2, 572	2, 433	2, 385
Share tenant	689	705	715	671	660
Renter 2	95	99	88	153	159
ATLANTIC COAST PLAIN					
Total	263	271	264	224	238
Wage laborer	96	97	104	85	81
Cropper	128	128	133	118	137
Share tenant	32	36	19	8	8
Renter 2	7	10	8	13	12

See footnotes at end of table.

Table 6.—Resident Families on Plantations, by Area and Type, 1934–1938—Con.

Area and type of family	1938	1937	1936	1935	1934
BLACK BELT (A)					
Total	263	263	260	234	238
Wage laborer	86	88	88	78	72
Cropper	153	157	155	135	145
Share tenant	16	9	9	16	15
Renter [2]	8	9	8	5	6
BLACK BELT (B)					
Total	109	109	112	106	113
Wage laborer	38	31	35	30	34
Cropper	55	62	61	48	50
Share tenant	5	5	5	13	12
Renter [2]	11	11	11	15	17
UPPER DELTA					
Total	1,830	1,826	1,799	1,667	1,591
Wage laborer	262	210	181	125	123
Cropper	1,091	1,117	1,108	1,108	1,045
Share tenant	471	490	509	421	408
Renter [2]	6	9	1	13	15
LOWER DELTA					
Total	323	313	300	261	266
Wage laborer	7	4	4	11	13
Cropper	211	208	194	125	122
Share tenant	42	41	42	59	62
Renter [2]	63	60	60	66	69
INTERIOR PLAIN					
Total	178	180	176	171	167
Wage laborer	59	72	46	39	38
Cropper	92	81	97	104	101
Share tenant	27	27	33	28	28
Renter [2]	—	—	—	—	—
MISSISSIPPI BLUFFS					
Total	425	406	400	455	451
Wage laborer	25	20	21	37	39
Cropper	336	321	316	301	294
Share tenant	64	65	63	76	79
Renter [2]	—	—	—	41	39
RED RIVER					
Total	308	304	292	277	275
Wage laborer	73	70	64	65	67
Cropper	231	230	221	203	199
Share tenant	4	4	7	9	9
Renter [2]	—	—	—	—	—
ARKANSAS RIVER					
Total	359	348	340	393	399
Wage laborer	28	26	25	61	67
Cropper	303	294	287	291	292
Share tenant	28	28	28	41	39
Renter [2]	—	—	—	—	1

[1] Excludes displaced families.
[2] Cash and standing.

Table 7.—Type of Tenants on Plantations, by Area, 1937 and 1934

Area	Total planta-tions	Number of plantations operated by—									
		Wage laborers		Croppers		Share tenants		Renters (cash and standing)		More than 1 type	
		1937	1934	1937	1934	1937	1934	1937	1934	1937	1934
All areas:											
Number	246	18	12	67	50	13	9	2	4	146	171
Percent	100.0	7.3	4.9	27.2	20.3	5.3	3.7	0.8	1.6	59.4	69.5
Atlantic Coast Plain	31	5	2	9	10	4	—	—	—	13	19
Black Belt (A)	31	3	2	3	2	—	—	—	—	25	27
Black Belt (B)	16	—	—	3	—	—	—	—	—	13	16
Upper Delta	79	4	3	26	23	6	6	—	—	43	47
Lower Delta	19	—	—	6	1	2	2	2	4	9	12
Interior Plain	17	3	—	2	4	—	—	—	—	12	13
Mississippi Bluffs	27	—	1	11	7	1	1	—	—	15	18
Red River	15	3	4	5	2	—	—	—	—	7	9
Arkansas River	11	—	—	2	1	—	—	—	—	9	10

Table 8.—Resident Families [1] per 1,000 Acres of Cropland, by Area and Type, 1937 and 1934

Area	Total planta-tions	Resident families per 1,000 acres of cropland									
		Total		Wage laborer		Cropper		Share tenant		Renter (cash and standing)	
		1937	1934	1937	1934	1937	1934	1937	1934	1937	1934
All areas	246	34.2	36.5	5.3	5.2	22.1	23.3	6.0	6.4	0.8	1.6
Atlantic Coast Plain	31	26.3	31.7	9.4	10.7	12.4	18.3	3.5	1.1	1.0	1.6
Black Belt (A)	31	24.1	25.3	8.1	7.7	14.4	15.4	0.8	1.6	0.8	0.6
Black Belt (B)	16	27.9	28.3	7.9	8.5	15.9	12.5	1.3	3.0	2.8	4.3
Upper Delta	79	40.0	37.2	4.6	2.9	24.4	24.4	10.8	9.5	0.2	0.4
Lower Delta	19	44.1	56.6	0.6	2.8	29.3	26.0	5.8	13.2	8.4	14.6
Interior Plain	17	26.9	28.8	10.7	6.6	12.2	17.4	4.0	4.8	—	—
Mississippi Bluffs	27	34.7	42.5	1.7	3.7	27.4	27.6	5.6	7.5	—	3.7
Red River	15	28.1	34.4	6.5	8.4	21.3	24.9	0.3	1.1	—	—
Arkansas River	11	33.8	41.1	2.5	6.9	28.6	30.2	2.7	4.0	—	—

[1] Excludes displaced families.

Table 9.—Type of Off-Plantation Labor, Transportation Arrangements, and Average [1] Miles Traveled, by Area, 1937

Area	Cotton chopping						Cotton picking					
	Local labor			Migratory labor			Local labor			Migratory labor		
	Plantations reporting transportation furnished by—		Average miles traveled	Plantations reporting transportation furnished by—		Average miles traveled	Plantations reporting transportation furnished by—		Average miles traveled	Plantations reporting transportation furnished by—		Average miles traveled
	Laborer	Operator		Laborer	Operator		Laborer	Operator		Laborer	Operator	
All areas	24	15	2	—	11	15	54	35	4	4	30	79
Atlantic Coast Plain	2	4	4	—	—	—	4	8	4	—	—	—
Black Belt (A)	5	6	2	—	—	—	11	7	2	—	2	28
Black Belt (B)	1	—	1	—	1	17	2	1	1	—	1	17
Upper Delta	12	2	2	—	6	15	23	12	3	3	11	77
Lower Delta	1	1	3	—	1	14	1	1	3	1	2	15
Interior Plain	1	—	2	—	1	13	1	—	2	—	1	12
Mississippi Bluffs	—	2	6	—	—	—	8	4	3	—	2	98
Red River	2	—	1	—	—	—	4	1	1	—	8	17
Arkansas River	—	—	—	—	2	15	—	1	4	—	3	22

[1] Arithmetic mean.

Table 10.—Crop Acres Handled by Tractors and Work Stock, by Area and Operation, 1937

Area	Percent of crop acreage in each operation handled by specified power																	
	Breaking					Seedbed preparation					Planting			Cultivating		
	Tractor	Number of work stock				Tractor	Number of work stock				Tractor	Number of work stock		Tractor	Number of work stock	
		4	3	2	1		4	3	2	1		2	1		2	1
All areas	38	3	1	49	9	34	3	2	37	24	19	24	57	21	37	42
Atlantic Coast Plain	10	1	—	79	10	14	3	—	29	54	5	7	88	5	32	63
Black Belt (A)	17	1	1	69	12	13	8	2	14	63	5	8	87	5	18	77
Black Belt (B)	7	—	—	47	46	2	—	—	36	62	—	—	100	—	6	94
Upper Delta	47	6	1	41	5	45	1	3	33	18	26	20	54	27	37	36
Lower Delta	32	—	—	38	30	28	1	2	35	34	10	39	51	15	34	51
Interior Plain	7	—	3	86	4	9	1	4	73	13	8	31	61	11	46	43
Mississippi Bluffs	56	—	—	26	18	43	—	5	48	4	14	12	74	27	43	30
Red River	64	—	—	36	—	57	—	—	43	—	45	41	14	44	40	16
Arkansas River	41	3	1	45	10	31	11	2	48	8	11	68	21	18	55	27

Table 11.—Operators' Long-Term Debts, by Type and Area, 1937 and 1934

Area	Total operators	Operators reporting debts	Debt per operator reporting debts	Percent of operators with debts reporting specified type of debt [1]					
				Mortgage	Bank	Merchant	Open account	Government	Other
All areas:									
1937	246	100	$11,914	82.0	8.0	1.0	2.0	9.0	4.0
1934	246	128	13,018	89.1	10.2	1.6	0.8	3.1	2.3
Atlantic Coast Plain:									
1937	31	10	4,759	50.0	10.0	—	10.0	20.0	10.0
1934	31	17	6,551	100.0	—	—	—	—	—
Black Belt (A):									
1937	31	20	5,115	95.0	15.0	5.0	—	—	—
1934	31	19	6,208	100.0	—	—	—	—	—
Black Belt (B):									
1937	16	3	3,233	—	66.7	—	—	33.3	—
1934	16	7	2,256	86.0	—	—	14.3	—	14.3
Upper Delta:									
1937	79	30	19,329	90.0	—	—	3.3	6.7	10.0
1934	79	36	16,061	91.6	5.6	2.8	—	2.8	—
Lower Delta:									
1937	19	5	3,370	20.0	20.0	—	—	60.0	—
1934	19	3	15,333	66.7	66.7	—	—	—	—
Interior Plain:									
1937	17	9	4,809	100.0	—	—	—	—	—
1934	17	13	8,292	92.3	7.7	—	—	—	7.7
Mississippi Bluffs:									
1937	27	9	12,111	88.9	11.1	—	—	—	—
1934	27	11	10,326	100.0	9.1	—	—	—	—
Red River:									
1937	15	6	23,583	83.3	—	—	—	16.7	—
1934	15	12	28,382	41.7	41.7	8.3	—	25.0	8.3
Arkansas River:									
1937	11	8	17,668	100.0	—	—	—	—	—
1934	11	10	23,504	90.0	20.0	—	—	—	—

[1] Some operators reported more than 1 type of debt.

Table 12.—Plantation Mortgages,[1] by Annual Rate of Interest and Type of Loan, 1937 and 1934

Annual rate of interest	Total mortgages		Type of loan					
			Government		Other		Unknown	
	1937	1934	1937	1934	1937	1934	1937	1934
Total	101	125	66	55	28	33	7	37
2.5 percent	1	—	—	—	1	—	—	—
3.0 percent	1	—	1	—	—	—	—	—
3.5 percent	12	3	11	2	1	—	—	1
4.0 percent	28	12	26	8	1	3	1	1
4.5 percent	4	10	4	8	—	—	—	2
5.0 percent	23	26	15	16	7	—	1	10
5.5 percent	2	18	1	14	1	1	—	3
6.0 percent	14	34	5	7	9	13	—	14
6.5 percent	1	2	1	—	—	1	—	1
7.0 percent	7	6	1	—	5	5	1	1
8.0 percent	2	11	—	—	2	9	—	2
Unknown	6	3	1	—	1	1	4	2
Average [2] rate	4.8	5.6	4.4	5.0	5.8	6.5	5.3	5.6

[1] Including other than first mortgages.
[2] Arithmetic mean.

Table 13.—Operators' Short-Term Credit, by Type[1] and Amount of Loans, Annual Rate of Interest, and Area, 1937 and 1934

Type of loan	All areas		Atlantic Coast Plain		Black Belt (A)		Black Belt (B)		Upper Delta		Lower Delta		Interior Plain		Mississippi Bluffs		Red River		Arkansas River	
	1937	1934	1937	1934	1937	1934	1937	1934	1937	1934	1937	1934	1937	1934	1937	1934	1937	1934	1937	1934
Total plantations	246		31		31		16		79		19		17		27		15		11	
Operators reporting short-term credit																				
Government	[2]38	30	7	3	2	1	3	4	14	5	—	—	1	6	3	1	3	3	5	7
Merchant	9	[3]13	2	3	2	1	1	—	1	4	—	3	2	—	—	—	—	1	1	—
Fertilizer	6	3	5	1	1	2	—	—	—	—	—	—	—	—	—	—	—	—	—	—
Bank	[4]65	[5]109	14	15	16	20	5	8	11	31	6	2	1	6	5	16	4	7	3	4
Total amount of loans																				
Government	$193,625	$69,779	$12,300	$4,000	$1,700	$300	$2,525	$5,100	$113,900	$22,050	—	—	$7,800	$7,445	$14,500	$3,400	$24,000	$4,875	$16,900	$22,609
Merchant	11,472	37,953	1,920	6,200	1,870	5,010	3,000	—	2,500	8,443	—	$8,300	200	—	—	2,000	—	8,000	—	1,982
Fertilizer	5,358	900	4,258	100	1,100	800	—	—	—	—	—	—	—	—	—	—	—	—	—	—
Bank	201,350	256,085	23,750	20,350	23,150	17,975	6,100	11,150	47,400	97,980	$24,250	750	2,000	6,505	7,900	57,275	30,800	28,500	36,000	15,600
Annual rate of interest																				
Government	11.9	11.8	8.6	11.0	10.1	8.0	8.4	12.7	12.0	13.6	—	—	10.0	11.9	12.0	10.9	12.8	19.6	14.3	9.0
Merchant	16.6	16.0	42.5	24.6	34.2	20.0	12.0	—	12.0	13.2	—	10.7	—	—	—	18.0	—	16.0	—	—
Fertilizer	22.9	30.0	14.0	61.7	73.6	26.3	—	—	20.4	16.6	—	—	—	—	—	—	—	—	—	—
Bank	16.0	15.3	15.3	13.7	16.8	17.8	12.3	19.4	20.4	16.6	14.4	14.9	12.0	19.8	18.5	13.6	11.7	12.9	16.6	15.1

[1] A small number of plantations reported current loans of other than the specified types.
[2] Exclusive of 2 plantations reporting Government loans but for which the amount of the loans was not available.
[3] Exclusive of 2 plantations reporting merchant loans but for which the amount of the interest was not available.
[4] Exclusive of 1 plantation reporting a bank loan but for which the amount of the loan was not available.
[5] Exclusive of 4 plantations reporting bank loans but for which the amount of the interest was not available.

Table 14.—Duration of Subsistence Advances and Annual Rate of Interest, by Area, 1937 and 1934

Area	Total operators reporting		Average [1] duration of advances (months)		Annual rate of interest [2]	
	1937	1934	1937	1934	1937	1934
All areas	[3] 206	[4] 224	3.4	3.6	35.7	39.6
Atlantic Coast Plain	24	27	4.2	4.6	15.7	16.7
Black Belt (A)	25	28	3.9	3.9	23.4	23.6
Black Belt (B)	16	16	4.2	3.6	11.8	22.8
Upper Delta	71	73	3.2	3.4	37.6	39.5
Lower Delta	7	15	3.1	3.3	48.2	49.3
Interior Plain	14	17	2.9	3.6	40.1	35.1
Mississippi Bluffs	27	27	3.1	3.1	46.6	47.7
Red River	12	10	3.0	3.8	32.5	31.6
Arkansas River	10	11	3.0	3.2	49.8	71.5

[1] Arithmetic mean.
[2] Secured by dividing interest paid×12 (months) by amount of loan×duration in months.
[3] Data not available for 1 plantation in the Upper Delta Area, 8 plantations in the Lower Delta Area, and 1 plantation in the Interior Plain Area.
[4] Data not available for 1 plantation in the Black Belt (A) Area.

Table 15.—Ratio of Prices Received for Cotton and Cottonseed and for All Agricultural Commodities to Prices Paid for Commodities Bought, 1924–1938

Year	Ratio of prices received to prices paid	
	Cotton and cottonseed	All agricultural commodities
1924	139	94
1925	113	99
1926	79	94
1927	84	91
1928	98	96
1929	94	95
1930	70	87
1931	51	70
1932	44	61
1933	59	64
1934	80	73
1935	81	86
1936	81	92
1937	73	93
1938	57	78

Source: Bureau of Agricultural Economics, The Agricultural Situation, Vol. 23, No. 4, U. S. Department of Agriculture, Washington, D. C., April 1939, p. 24.

Table 16.—Investment per Plantation and per Crop Acre for Land, Buildings, Livestock, and Machinery, by Area, 1937 and 1934

Area	Total plantations		Investment per plantation									
			Total		Land		Buildings		Livestock		Machinery	
	1937	1934	1937	1934	1937	1934	1937	1934	1937	1934	1937	1934
All areas	[1] 245	[2] 241	$37,504	$31,378	$27,874	$23,484	$4,814	$4,366	$2,947	$1,996	$1,869	$1,532
Atlantic Coast Plain	31	31	25,305	16,749	18,948	11,550	3,318	3,344	1,986	1,310	1,053	545
Black Belt (A)	31	31	19,433	18,147	12,395	12,087	3,558	3,247	2,620	1,640	860	1,173
Black Belt (B)	16	14	10,911	12,874	7,177	8,649	2,044	2,464	1,302	1,409	388	352
Upper Delta	79	78	55,044	43,676	41,184	32,857	7,895	6,280	3,520	2,332	2,445	2,207
Lower Delta	18	19	31,318	23,261	25,621	18,196	2,835	2,455	1,803	1,586	1,059	1,024
Interior Plain	17	17	17,217	22,220	12,674	17,139	1,724	2,632	1,772	1,491	1,047	958
Mississippi Bluffs	27	27	31,411	24,287	23,765	19,157	2,828	2,500	2,859	1,708	1,959	922
Red River	15	15	44,845	52,855	31,474	38,616	4,053	6,729	5,530	3,903	3,788	3,607
Arkansas River	11	9	81,931	69,443	63,524	56,587	8,395	7,081	5,229	3,082	4,783	2,693
Percent distribution												
All areas	[1] 245	[2] 241	100.0	100.0	74.3	74.8	12.8	13.9	7.9	6.4	5.0	4.9
Atlantic Coast Plain	31	31	100.0	100.0	74.9	68.9	13.1	20.0	7.8	7.8	4.2	3.3
Black Belt (A)	31	31	100.0	100.0	63.8	66.6	18.3	17.9	13.5	9.0	4.4	6.5
Black Belt (B)	16	14	100.0	100.0	65.8	67.3	18.7	19.1	11.9	10.9	3.6	2.7
Upper Delta	79	78	100.0	100.0	74.9	75.2	14.3	14.4	6.4	5.3	4.4	5.1
Lower Delta	18	19	100.0	100.0	81.7	78.2	9.1	10.6	5.8	6.8	3.4	4.4
Interior Plain	17	17	100.0	100.0	73.6	77.2	10.0	11.8	10.3	6.7	6.1	4.3
Mississippi Bluffs	27	27	100.0	100.0	75.7	78.9	9.0	10.3	9.1	7.0	6.2	3.8
Red River	15	15	100.0	100.0	70.3	73.1	9.0	12.7	12.3	7.4	8.4	6.8
Arkansas River	11	9	100.0	100.0	77.6	81.5	10.2	10.2	6.4	4.4	5.8	3.9
Investment per crop acre												
All areas	[1] 245	[2] 241	$79	$75	$58	$56	$10	$10	$6	$5	$5	$4
Atlantic Coast Plain	31	31	76	69	57	47	10	14	6	5	4	3
Black Belt (A)	31	31	56	60	36	40	10	11	8	5	2	4
Black Belt (B)	16	14	45	52	30	35	8	10	5	5	2	2
Upper Delta	79	78	95	81	71	61	14	12	6	4	4	4
Lower Delta	18	19	84	93	69	73	7	10	5	6	3	4
Interior Plain	17	17	43	65	32	50	7	8	4	4	3	3
Mississippi Bluffs	27	27	72	62	54	49	6	6	7	4	5	3
Red River	15	15	62	99	44	72	6	13	8	7	5	7
Arkansas River	11	9	87	79	68	64	9	8	5	4	5	3

[1] Data not available for 1 plantation in the Lower Delta Area.
[2] Data not available for 2 plantations in the Black Belt (B) Area, 1 plantation in the Upper Delta Area, and 2 plantations in the Arkansas River Area.

Table 17.—Gross Income From Cash Receipts per Plantation and per Crop Acre, by Source of Income and Area, 1937 and 1934

Item	All areas 1937	All areas 1934	Atlantic Coast Plain 1937	Atlantic Coast Plain 1934	Black Belt (A) 1937	Black Belt (A) 1934	Black Belt (B) 1937	Black Belt (B) 1934	Upper Delta 1937	Upper Delta 1934	Lower Delta 1937	Lower Delta 1934	Interior Plain 1937	Interior Plain 1934	Mississippi Bluffs 1937	Mississippi Bluffs 1934	Red River 1937	Red River 1934	Arkansas River 1937	Arkansas River 1934
Total plantations	246		31		31		16		79		19		17		27		15		11	
Crop acres per plantation	477	417	331	243	350	303	243	249	579	542	373	249	397	340	434	392	718	535	940	880
									Gross income from cash receipts per plantation											
Total	$13,679	$9,974	$8,928	$6,887	$5,567	$4,869	$3,127	$4,237	$21,326	$14,474	$7,693	$5,124	$6,242	$5,775	$12,804	$8,844	$20,766	$15,088	$24,665	$19,746
Cotton	10,721	7,437	3,171	2,732	3,042	2,828	2,364	3,278	18,524	11,667	6,206	3,724	4,837	4,145	10,797	7,197	16,219	11,494	18,976	15,902
Lint	8,800	5,897	2,796	2,268	2,597	2,350	2,128	2,689	15,090	9,117	5,462	2,897	3,863	3,276	8,520	5,695	13,113	9,181	15,938	12,917
Cottonseed	1,921	1,540	375	464	445	478	236	589	3,434	2,550	744	827	974	869	2,277	1,502	3,106	2,313	3,038	2,985
AAA payments	1,237	1,123	582	605	404	492	346	399	1,403	1,594	606	575	1,082	905	1,633	968	2,451	1,711	4,231	2,882
Feed sales	194	189	161	121	108	165	7	24	308	314	—	239	100	48	176	197	367	13	267	168
Corn	113	122	17	93	88	87	3	19	184	169	—	239	100	47	176	197	225	13	62	9
Hay	55	65	44	22	20	78	4	5	120	145	—	—	—	1	—	—	89	—	205	159
Other	26	2	100	6	—	—	—	—	4	—	—	—	—	—	—	—	53	—	—	—
Other crop sales	914	716	4,646	3,236	1,181	1,029	177	118	509	466	21	12	37	128	—	—	—	21	15	226
Peanuts	161	171	554	778	726	581	—	—	—	—	—	—	—	—	—	—	—	—	—	—
Tobacco	672	465	3,839	2,257	194	241	—	—	—	—	—	—	—	—	—	—	—	—	—	—
Other	81	80	[1] 253	[1] 201	[2] 261	[2] 207	[3] 177	[3] 118	[4] 509	466	[5] 21	12	[6] 37	[6] 128	—	—	—	[7] 21	[8] 15	[8] 226
Livestock products sales	435	230	298	104	775	215	161	196	320	79	480	150	142	437	39	69	1,631	1,616	796	86
Other receipts	178	279	70	89	57	140	72	222	262	354	380	424	44	112	159	413	98	233	380	482
Cash rent and miscellaneous	53	125	28	36	18	90	47	183	51	124	325	303	—	—	—	262	—	63	46	16
Interest and commissions	125	154	42	53	39	50	25	39	211	230	55	121	44	112	159	151	98	170	334	466

See footnotes at end of table.

Table 17.—Gross Income From Cash Receipts per Plantation and per Crop Acre, by Source of Income and Area, 1937 and 1934—Continued

Item	All areas		Atlantic Coast Plain		Black Belt (A)		Black Belt (B)		Upper Delta		Lower Delta		Interior Plain		Mississippi Bluffs		Red River		Arkansas River	
	1937	1934	1937	1934	1937	1934	1937	1934	1937	1934	1937	1934	1937	1934	1937	1934	1937	1934	1937	1934
	Percent distribution																			
Total	100.0	100.0	100.0	100.0	100.0	100.0	100.0	100.0	100.0	100.0	100.0	100.0	100.0	100.0	100.0	100.0	100.0	100.0	100.0	100.0
Cotton	78.4	74.5	35.5	39.6	54.7	58.1	75.6	77.4	86.9	80.7	80.7	72.7	77.5	71.8	84.3	81.4	78.0	76.3	76.9	80.6
AAA payments	9.0	11.3	6.5	8.8	7.3	10.1	11.1	9.4	6.6	11.0	7.9	11.2	17.3	15.7	12.8	10.9	11.8	11.3	17.2	14.6
Feed sales	1.4	1.9	1.8	1.8	1.9	3.4	0.2	0.6	1.4	2.2	—	4.7	1.6	0.8	1.4	2.2	1.8	0.1	1.1	0.9
Other crop sales	6.7	7.2	52.1	47.0	21.2	21.1	5.7	2.8	2.4	3.2	0.3	0.2	0.6	2.2	—	—	—	0.1	0.1	1.1
Livestock products sales	3.2	2.3	3.3	1.5	13.9	4.4	5.1	4.6	1.5	0.5	6.2	2.9	2.3	7.6	0.3	0.8	7.9	10.7	3.2	0.4
Other receipts	1.3	2.8	0.8	1.3	1.0	2.9	2.3	5.2	1.2	2.4	4.9	8.3	0.7	1.9	1.2	4.7	0.5	1.5	1.5	2.4
Gross income per crop acre	$29	$24	$27	$28	$16	$16	$13	$17	$37	$27	$21	$21	$16	$17	$30	$23	$29	$28	$26	$22

1 Major sources: Wheat, sweet potatoes, and soybeans, and watermelons in 1934.
2 Major sources: Pecans, vegetables, orchard, and sugar cane.
3 Major sources: Wheat, cowpeas for seed, and soybeans.
4 Major sources: Pecans, certified seed, and cowpeas for seed.
5 Major sources: Pecans and vegetables.
6 Major sources: Cowpeas for seed and orchard, and strawberries in 1934.
7 Major source: Cowpeas for seed.
8 Major sources: Cowpeas for seed and pecans.

Table 18.—Gross Income for the One-Fourth of the Plantations in Each Area With the Highest and the Lowest Gross Income per Plantation, by Area, 1937 and 1934

Area	Total plantations in each income group 1937 and 1934	Gross income for one-fourth of plantations in each area with highest gross income per plantation						Gross income for one-fourth of plantations in each area with lowest gross income per plantation					
		Per plantation		Per family [1]		Per crop acre		Per plantation		Per family [1]		Per crop acre	
		1937	1934	1937	1934	1937	1934	1937	1934	1937	1934	1937	1934
All areas	63	$30,154	$21,322	$982	$707	$34	$27	$3,715	$2,915	$548	$395	$21	$16
Atlantic Coast Plain	8	17,305	13,268	1,610	1,516	41	49	2,523	2,049	360	349	10	11
Black Belt (A)	8	11,398	9,904	786	890	16	19	1,915	1,568	374	267	13	10
Black Belt (B)	4	5,489	7,432	549	803	18	21	1,264	1,652	241	245	13	9
Upper Delta	20	45,179	30,185	1,020	696	42	29	6,255	4,193	834	541	32	24
Lower Delta	5	19,644	13,751	646	573	29	28	794	746	132	113	13	7
Interior Plain	4	17,259	11,627	842	705	21	19	1,340	1,789	315	298	10	13
Mississippi Bluffs	7	31,940	22,606	1,012	623	38	26	1,711	1,605	352	321	13	13
Red River	4	52,268	31,932	1,340	824	35	31	5,168	5,316	544	519	20	18
Arkansas River	3	48,211	41,084	742	511	27	21	8,805	6,953	660	372	26	19

[1] Excludes resident families without crops.

Table 19.—Current Expenses per Plantation, by Area, 1937 and 1934

Item	All areas		Atlantic Coast Plain		Black Belt (A)		Black Belt (B)		Upper Delta		Lower Delta		Interior Plain		Mississippi Bluffs		Red River		Arkansas River	
	1937	1934	1937	1934	1937	1934	1937	1934	1937	1934	1937	1934	1937	1934	1937	1934	1937	1934	1937	1934
Total plantations	246		31		31		16		79		19		17		27		15		11	
Current expenses per plantation	$6,006	$4,285	$3,339	$2,438	$2,652	$2,249	$2,209	$2,233	$9,586	$6,403	$2,990	$1,471	$2,301	$2,297	$4,784	$3,562	$10,745	$8,258	$10,262	$7,288
Labor	2,166	1,319	898	641	747	723	484	514	3,749	2,014	984	319	909	609	1,461	748	4,460	3,054	3,396	2,944
Regular wage laborers[1]	658	631	571	454	467	385	322	361	1,046	799	364	179	442	226	303	393	751	1,543	706	1,766
Seasonal wage laborers	1,037	226	70	97	140	101	10	43	2,215	378	451	97	294	14	899	232	1,707	319	926	513
Cotton chopping	120	85	11	38	16	22	2	19	159	159	105	39	36	7	79	71	270	77	145	203
Cotton picking	917	141	59	59	124	79	8	24	1,981	219	346	58	258	7	820	161	1,437	242	781	310
Tenant occasional	364	296	191	50	75	66	113	61	310	621	17	13	173	353	228	109	1,846	247	1,632	605
Miscellaneous	107	166	66	40	65	171	39	49	178	216	152	30		16	31	14	156	945	132	60
Repairs	497	342	316	197	228	197	378	156	805	514	269	140	99	347	224	247	943	587	793	440
Dwelling	215	121	110	82	119	96	102	106	465	170	78	51	63	101	78	146	27	142	207	39
Barns, fences, and implements	282	221	206	115	109	101	276	50	340	344	191	89	36	246	146	101	916	445	586	401
Feed for livestock	86	213	41	29	65	90	54	86	112	339	118	47	31	239	101	23	445	478	468	611
Veterinary fees	21	16	19	10	12	9	3	1	31	19	14	5	6	12	4		64	45	35	13
Seed	137	129	128	42	74	48	45	76	175	240	81	21	30	16	87	102	169	210	455	190
Tractor expenses	197	130	42		32	16	2	4	319	238	72	41		213	151	51	548	289	619	409
Fertilizer	637	435	1,121	947	723	513	880	852	608	331	192	87	222	66	939	451	177	222	171	112
Wage crops	242	133	362	276	258	192	316	327	254	87	30	3	147	147	329	17	107	222	158	112
Tenant crops	395	302	759	671	465	321	564	525	354	244	162	84	75	4	610	434	70		13	
Poison for pest control	19	69		4		4			51	174	5	5			11	91		33	24	
Ginning	1,065	551	234	145	231	298	142	255	1,938	873	670	248	556	295	1,067	609	1,492	755	1,727	1,030
Rent	306	292	94	130	76	62	12	123	464	439	10	7	62	132	37	225	2,003	1,130	82	334
Real estate	605	613	322	234	285	175	152	114	939	1,021	432	404	204	281	617	579	725	1,046	1,292	1,088
Insurance	119	106	99	31	68	31	41	33	161	218	98	48	23	30	83	67	133	67	913	149
Taxes	486	507	223	203	217	144	111	81	778	803	334	356	181	251	534	512	592	943	245	939
Interest	211	122	118	43	60	69	57	51	394	157	143	52	91	29	183	321	164	134	955	109
Miscellaneous	59	54	6		119	45		1	1	44		95		59		47		275		8
Current expenses per crop acre	$13	$10	$10	$10	$8	$7	$9	$9	$17	$12	$8	$6	$6	$6	$11	$9	$15	$15	$11	$8

[1] Includes nonresident laborers.

Table 20.—Financial Summary [1] per Plantation and per Crop Acre, by Area, 1937 and 1934

Item	All acres		Atlantic Coast Plain		Black Belt (A)		Black Belt (B)		Upper Delta		Lower Delta		Interior Plain		Mississippi Bluffs		Red River		Arkansas River	
	1937	1934	1937	1934	1937	1934	1937	1934	1937	1934	1937	1934	1937	1934	1937	1934	1937	1934	1937	1934
Total plantations	246		31		31		16		79		19		17		27		15		11	
Crop acres per plantation	477	417	331	243	350	303	243	249	579	542	373	249	397	340	434	392	718	535	940	880
Financial summary per plantation																				
Investment	$37,504	$31,378	$25,305	$16,749	$19,433	$18,147	$10,911	$12,874	$55,044	$43,676	$31,318	$23,261	$17,217	$22,220	$31,411	$24,287	$44,845	$52,855	$31,931	$69,443
Gross cash income	13,679	9,974	8,928	6,887	5,567	4,809	3,127	4,237	21,326	14,474	7,693	5,124	6,242	5,775	12,804	8,844	20,766	15,088	24,665	19,746
Current expenses	6,006	4,285	3,339	2,438	2,652	2,249	2,209	2,233	9,586	6,403	2,990	1,471	2,301	2,297	4,784	3,562	10,745	8,258	10,262	7,288
Net cash income	7,673	5,689	5,589	4,449	2,915	2,620	918	2,004	11,740	8,071	4,703	3,653	3,941	3,478	8,020	5,282	10,021	6,830	14,403	12,458
Financial summary per crop acre																				
Investment	$79	$75	$76	$69	$56	$60	$45	$52	$95	$81	$84	$93	$43	$65	$72	$62	$62	$99	$87	$79
Gross cash income	29	24	27	28	16	16	13	17	37	27	21	21	16	17	30	23	29	28	26	22
Current expenses	13	10	10	10	8	7	9	9	17	12	8	6	6	7	11	9	15	15	11	8
Net cash income	16	14	17	18	8	9	4	8	20	15	13	15	10	10	18	13	14	13	15	14

[1] Based on appendix tables 1, 16, 17, and 19.

Table 21.—Operator's Gross Cash Income From Cash Receipts per Plantation, by Area and Source of Income, 1937 and 1934

Area	Total planta- tions	Gross cash income per plantation				
		Total	Crop sales	AAA payments	Livestock products sales	Other receipts [1]
All areas:						
1937	246	$8,328	$6,882	$833	$435	$178
1934	246	5,908	4,420	979	230	279
Atlantic Coast Plain:						
1937	31	4,837	4,082	387	298	70
1934	31	4,257	3,570	494	104	89
Black Belt (A):						
1937	31	3,427	2,286	309	775	57
1934	31	3,219	2,425	439	215	140
Black Belt (B):						
1937	16	2,130	1,645	252	161	72
1934	16	3,007	2,225	364	196	222
Upper Delta:						
1937	79	12,909	11,317	1,010	320	262
1934	79	8,140	6,332	1,375	79	354
Lower Delta:						
1937	19	4,567	3,219	488	480	380
1934	19	2,970	1,862	534	150	424
Interior Plain:						
1937	17	3,659	2,875	598	142	44
1934	17	3,526	2,175	802	437	112
Mississippi Bluffs:						
1937	27	7,596	6,372	1,026	39	159
1934	27	4,624	3,327	815	69	413
Red River:						
1937	15	14,279	10,890	1,660	1,631	98
1934	15	10,539	7,135	1,555	1,616	233
Arkansas River:						
1937	11	17,208	13,308	2,724	796	380
1934	11	12,791	9,615	2,608	86	482

[1] Cash rent, interest, commissions, and miscellaneous.

Table 22.—Operator's Net Cash Gain or Loss per Plantation, 1937 and 1934

Net cash gain or loss	Total plantations		Net cash gain or loss per plantation	
	1937	1934	1937	1934
Total	[1] 245	246	$3,590	$2,528
Loss	20	18	−741	−468
$500 or more	8	7	−1,636	−869
Less than $500	12	11	−144	−212
Gain	225	228	4,331	2,996
Less than $500	24	29	260	323
$500–$999	32	43	759	703
$1,000–$1,499	19	23	1,211	1,202
$1,500–$1,999	17	22	1,574	1,676
$2,000–$2,499	21	23	2,163	2,221
$2,500–$4,999	45	51	3,574	3,563
$5,000 or more	67	37	10,268	9,362

[1] Data not available for 1 plantation in the Upper Delta Area.

Table 23.—Operator's Financial Summary [1] per Plantation and per Crop Acre, by Area, 1937 and 1934

Item	All areas		Atlantic Coast Plain		Black Belt (A)		Black Belt (B)		Upper Delta		Lower Delta		Interior Plain		Mississippi Bluffs		Red River		Arkansas River	
	1937	1934	1937	1934	1937	1934	1937	1934	1937	1934	1937	1934	1937	1934	1937	1934	1937	1934	1937	1934
Total plantations	246		31		31		16		79		19		17		27		15		11	
Crop acres per plantation	477	417	331	243	350	303	243	249	579	542	373	249	397	340	434	392	718	535	940	830
Financial summary per plantation																				
Gross cash income	$8,328	$5,908	$4,837	$4,257	$3,427	$3,219	$2,130	$3,007	$12,909	$8,140	$4,567	$2,970	$3,659	$3,526	$7,596	$4,624	$14,279	$10,539	$17,208	$12,791
Current expenses	4,738	3,380	2,931	2,087	2,049	1,786	1,915	1,894	7,293	4,862	2,145	1,154	1,889	1,968	3,472	2,204	9,681	7,743	9,382	6,382
Net cash income	3,590	2,528	1,906	2,170	1,378	1,433	215	1,113	5,616	3,278	2,422	1,816	1,770	1,558	4,124	2,420	4,598	2,796	7,826	6,409
Financial summary per crop acre																				
Gross cash income	$18	$14	$15	$18	$10	$11	$9	$12	$23	$15	$12	$12	$9	$11	$18	$12	$19	$19	$18	$14
Current expenses	10	8	9	9	6	6	8	8	13	9	6	5	5	6	8	6	13	14	10	7
Net income	8	6	6	9	4	5	1	4	10	6	6	7	4	5	10	6	6	5	8	7

[1] Based on table 25 and appendix tables 1 and 21.

Table 24.—Net Cash Income from Crops [1] per Tenant Family [2] and Percent of Total Plantation Crop Acres in Cotton, 1937 and 1934

Net cash income per tenant family	Total plantations reporting [3]		Percent of crop acres in cotton							
			Less than 30		30–49		50–69		70 or more	
	1937	1934	1937	1934	1937	1934	1937	1934	1937	1934
Total	[4] 199	224	58	79	89	96	47	41	5	8
Less than $50	1	2	1	1	—	1	—	—	—	—
$50–$99	21	19	16	10	5	7	—	2	—	—
$100–$149	29	37	13	13	13	17	3	7	—	—
$150–$199	33	54	10	16	17	24	5	12	1	2
$200–$249	38	44	7	12	23	20	5	9	3	3
$250–$299	22	32	4	8	9	14	9	7	—	3
$300–$399	36	13	2	5	16	6	17	2	1	—
$400–$499	12	6	4	1	4	5	4	—	—	—
$500 or more	7	17	1	13	2	2	4	2	—	—
Median income	$220	$200	$146	$198	$221	$198	$309	$198	$225	$233

[1] Excludes plantations on which 50 percent or more of the gross cash income from crop sales was derived from tobacco and/or peanuts.
[2] Cropper and share tenant families only.
[3] Excludes plantations operated by wage laborers only.
[4] Data not available for 2 plantations.

Table 25.—Reasons of Out-of-School Negro Children for Not Being in School [1]

Reason	Number	Percent
Total	[2] 1,540	100.0
Distance	103	6.7
Working	797	51.7
Grade completed	108	7.0
Lack of books	43	2.8
Lack of clothes	109	7.1
Personal illness	43	2.8
Parents' illness	1	0.1
Married	45	2.9
Indifference	101	6.6
Physical handicap	17	1.1
Other	173	11.2

[1] From a study made in 28 counties in 6 Southern States.
[2] Median age=14.2 years.

Source: Caliver, Ambrose, *Availability of Education to Negroes in Rural Communities*, Bulletin, 1935, No. 12, U. S. Department of the Interior, Office of Education, Washington, D. C., 1936, p. 17.

Table 26.—Volumes per Capita in Public Libraries and Percent of Rural Population Residing in Local Public Library Districts in 12 Southern States, 1934

State	Volumes per capita in public libraries [1]	Percent of rural population residing in local public library districts [2]
Alabama	0. 16	15. 4
Arkansas	0. 10	2. 9
Georgia	0. 19	8. 7
Kentucky	0. 25	16. 3
Louisiana	0. 19	12. 3
Mississippi	0. 10	25. 1
North Carolina	0. 20	30. 3
Oklahoma	0. 32	3. 3
South Carolina	0. 12	24. 9
Tennessee	0. 29	16. 8
Texas	0. 23	7. 1
Virginia	0. 67	7. 6

[1] United States volumes per capita (including District of Columbia)=0.82.
[2] United States percent=11.4.

Source: Wilson, Louis R., *The Geography of Reading*, American Library Association and The University of Chicago Press, Chicago, Ill., 1938, pp. 28 and 48.

Table 27.—Circulation of 47 National Magazines, 1931, and of 42 Farm Publications, 1928, per 1,000 Population

State	Circulation of 47 national magazines per 1,000 population, 1931 [1]	Circulation of 42 farm publications per 1,000 population, 1928 [2]
Alabama	124	86. 1
Arkansas	136	108. 2
Georgia	141	82. 1
Kentucky	166	90. 2
Louisiana	150	57. 5
Mississippi	101	104. 0
North Carolina	138	105. 0
Oklahoma	222	148. 3
South Carolina	114	82. 0
Tennessee	174	84. 5
Texas	225	98. 0
Virginia	204	115. 1

[1] United States circulation per 1,000 population (including District of Columbia)=312.
[2] United States circulation per 1,000 population (including District of Columbia)=104.7.

Source: Wilson, Louis R., *The Geography of Reading*, American Library Association and The University of Chicago Press, Chicago, Ill., 1938, pp. 230 and 234.

Appendix B

LIST OF TABLES

TEXT TABLES

Table   *Page*

1. Plantations enumerated, by area, 1937 and 1934 _____ XII
2. Operators with other occupations, by area, 1937 and 1934 _____ 2
3. Resident and absentee operators, by area, 1937 and 1934 _____ 2
4. Organization of land per plantation, by area, 1937 and 1934 _____ 4
5. Organization of cropland per plantation, 1937 and 1934 _____ 5
6. Organization of cropland per plantation, by tenure and area, 1937 and 1934 _____ 6
7. Plantation livestock, by area, 1937 and 1934 _____ 10
8. Resident families per plantation, by area and type, 1937 and 1934 ____ 13
9. Color of tenants on plantations, by area, 1937 and 1934 _____ 15
10. Cotton acreage chopped or picked by off-plantation labor, by area and tenure of operator, 1937 _____ 16
11. Power per plantation and per 1,000 acres of cropland, by area, 1937 and 1934 _____ 17
12. Type of power used on plantations, by area, 1937 _____ 18
13. Number of tractors per plantation, by area, 1937 _____ 19
14. Factors retarding mechanization as reported by operators, 1937 _____ 20
15. Operators' long-term debts, by type, 1937 and 1934 _____ 24
16. Operators' short-term credit, by type, amount, and duration of loan and annual rate of interest, 1937 and 1934 _____ 25
17. Operators' short-term credit, by number of resident families, 1937 and 1934 _____ 26
18. Practice of operators in granting subsistence advances, by area, 1937 and 1934 _____ 28
19. Investment per plantation and per crop acre for land, buildings, livestock, and machinery, 1937 and 1934 _____ 30
20. Gross income from cash receipts per plantation, by source of income, 1937 and 1934 _____ 31
21. Gross income for the one-fourth of the plantations in each area with the highest and lowest gross income per plantation, 1937 and 1934 __ 33
22. Current expenses per plantation, 1937 and 1934 _____ 34
23. Net cash income per plantation and per crop acre, by area, 1937 and 1934 _____ 36

Table		Page
24.	Operator's gross cash income from cash receipts per plantation, by source of income, 1937 and 1934	40
25.	Operator's current expenses per plantation, by area, 1937 and 1934	41
26.	Operator's net cash income per plantation, by area, 1937 and 1934	41
27.	Net income per tenant family, by area, 1937 and 1934	44
28.	Net cash income per cropper family, by area, 1937 and 1934	45
29.	Changes in farm population and in farm operators in Southern regions, 1930 to 1935	49
30	Changes in farm operators in Southern cotton regions, by tenure, 1930 to 1935	49
31.	Federal aid per capita, January 1933–March 1938	52
32.	Households receiving public assistance in the South, November 1933–November 1938	53
33.	Food consumption of low-income rural families in 5 Southern counties, January–March 1939	57
34.	Plumbing facilities reported by white farm operator families in 8 counties in North Carolina and South Carolina, by income, 1935–36	59
35.	School attainment of heads of open country families in the Eastern Cotton Area receiving general relief, by color, October 1935	65
36.	Percent of the open country general relief population 7 through 17 years of age in the Eastern Cotton Area attending school, by color, October 1935	65
37.	Negro rural children who are over-age for their grade, by distance to school	66
38.	Farms in 12 Southern States receiving central-station service, June 30, 1939	68

SUPPLEMENTARY TABLES

1.	Crop acres per plantation, by area, 1934–1938	79
2.	Crop acres on plantations, by area, 1937 and 1934	79
3.	Organization of cropland per plantation, by area, 1937 and 1934	80
4.	Cotton acreage on plantations, by area, 1937 and 1934	81
5.	Yield of lint cotton per acre, by type of tenants and area, 1937 and 1934	81
6.	Resident families on plantations, by area and type, 1934–1938	81
7.	Type of tenants on plantations, by area, 1937 and 1934	83
8.	Resident families per 1,000 acres of cropland, by area and type, 1937 and 1934	83
9.	Type of off-plantation labor, transportation arrangements, and average miles traveled, by area, 1937	84
10.	Crop acres handled by tractors and work stock, by area and operation, 1937	84
11.	Operators' long-term debts, by type and area, 1937 and 1934	85
12.	Plantation mortgages, by annual rate of interest and type of loan, 1937 and 1934	85
13.	Operators' short-term credit, by type and amount of loans, annual rate of interest, and area, 1937 and 1934	86
14.	Duration of subsistence advances and annual rate of interest, by area 1937 and 1934	87
15.	Ratio of prices received for cotton and cottonseed and for all agricultural commodities to prices paid for commodities bought, 1924–1938	87

Table   *Page*

16. Investment per plantation and per crop acre for land, buildings, livestock, and machinery, by area, 1937 and 1934_____   88

17. Gross income from cash receipts per plantation and per crop acre, by source of income and area, 1937 and 1934_____   89

18. Gross income for the one-fourth of the plantations in each area with the highest and the lowest gross income per plantation, by area, 1937 and 1934_____   91

19. Current expenses per plantation, by area, 1937 and 1934_____   92

20. Financial summary per plantation and per crop acre, by area, 1937 and 1934_____   93

21. Operator's gross cash income from cash receipts per plantation, by area and source of income, 1937 and 1934_____   94

22. Operator's net cash gain or loss per plantation, 1937 and 1934_____   94

23. Operator's financial summary per plantation and per crop acre, by area, 1937 and 1934_____   95

24. Net cash income from crops per tenant family and percent of total plantation crop acres in cotton, 1937 and 1934_____   96

25. Reasons of out-of-school Negro children for not being in school_____   96

26. Volumes per capita in public libraries and percent of rural population residing in local public library districts in 12 Southern States, 1934__   97

27. Circulation of 47 national magazines, 1931, and of 42 farm publications, 1928, per 1,000 population_____   97

Appendix C

METHOD AND SCOPE OF THE STUDY

IN ORDER to analyze recent changes in the organization and operation of the plantations in the Eastern Cotton Area for which the 1934 operations were surveyed,[1] a restudy was made based on plantation operations for the crop year 1937 and the current situation at the time of the field enumeration during the summer of 1938. In this resurvey special emphasis was placed on changes in labor force and in mechanization. A total of 320 plantations scattered through 31 counties of Arkansas, Georgia, Louisiana, Mississippi, and North Carolina was enumerated (table A). Alabama, included in 1934, was completely omitted in 1937 for the reason that its principal farming areas are similar to those sampled in Georgia and Mississippi. For purposes of analysis 246 plantations, surveyed as of both years, were utilized.

The definition of a plantation in both studies is a tract owned or leased by one individual or corporation and operated under one management by five or more families, including that of the resident landlord. This conforms in general to the definition adopted in the 1910 Census,[2] when the last comprehensive enumeration of plantations was made.

The sample was classified into nine areas which conformed to the areas delimited in the earlier survey after the elimination of the Upper Piedmont and Muscle Shoals Areas. These two areas were omitted as the resurvey was deliberately weighted toward areas in which mechanization is becoming a more or less significant factor. The eliminations also weight the 1937 sample somewhat toward the larger plantations with high per acre yields.

---

[1] Woofter, T. J., Jr. and Others, *Landlord and Tenant on the Cotton Plantation*, Research Monograph V, Division of Social Research, Works Progress Administration, Washington, D. C., 1936.

[2] *Ibid.* For exceptions to the general definition, see p. 245.

Table A.—Plantations Enumerated, by County, 1937 and 1934

State and county	1937	1934	Matched schedules
Total	320	646	246
Alabama	—	154	—
Bibb	—	18	—
Bullock	—	25	—
Calhoun	—	12	—
Elmore	—	18	—
Hale	—	29	—
Lauderdale	—	22	—
Lowndes	—	30	—
Arkansas	57	89	35
Chicot	5	—	—
Crittenden	7	12	—
Jefferson	8	14	6
Lincoln	3	7	2
Lonoke	5	6	3
Miller	11	18	9
Phillips	12	20	7
Pulaski	—	2	—
Woodruff	6	10	4
Georgia	61	115	41
Carroll	—	12	—
Dodge	6	9	3
Hancock	9	13	6
Jenkins	12	18	7
McDuffie	13	20	10
Madison	—	12	—
Mitchell	12	18	8
Webster	9	13	7
Louisiana	51	68	49
Caddo	6	10	6
Concordia	17	19	16
Lincoln	7	10	6
Tensas	14	19	14
Webster	7	10	7
Mississippi	100	174	90
Adams	15	25	13
Carroll	10	17	10
Clay	6	14	6
Coahoma	10	22	19
Quitman	14	20	12
Warren	10	25	6
Washington	17	21	17
Yazoo	18	30	17
North Carolina	51	46	31
Anson	14	13	10
Cumberland	12	12	8
Edgecombe	21	17	13
Iredell	4	4	—

The representativeness of the Eastern Cotton Area sample for 1937 is directly related to the representativeness of the sample for 1934. Available checks and appraisals by persons familiar with the areas surveyed indicate that the 1934 sample, carefully selected on the basis of cotton production, percent tenancy, per capita income from agriculture, and the value of farm land per acre, formed a reliable basis for analyzing production factors and tenant relations on cotton plantations.[3] Omitting the four counties of Pulaski, Ark., Carroll and Madison, Ga., and Iredell, N. C., and the seven Alabama counties for which no schedules were included in the resurvey,[4] the distribution of plantations, by area, utilized in the present analysis was

[3] *Ibid.*, pp. 243–246.

[4] Chicot, Ark., was also omitted because no plantations were enumerated in this county in 1934.

found to be similar to the larger sample of the 1934 study (table B). Moreover, by using the same plantations as the basis for the comparative analysis of plantation organization and operation, it appears that the observed differences reflect actual changes in organization and operation occurring among the larger agricultural units of the Southeast.

Table B.—Matched Plantations for 1937 and 1934 and Plantations Enumerated in 1934, by Area

Area	Matched plantations, 1937 and 1934		1934 enumeration [1]
	Number	Percent	Percent
All areas	246	100.0	100.0
Atlantic Coast Plain	31	12.6	12.1
Black Belt (A)	31	12.6	14.1
Black Belt (B)	16	6.5	5.6
Upper Delta	79	32.1	28.8
Lower Delta	19	7.7	10.8
Interior Plain	17	6.9	6.5
Mississippi Bluffs	27	11.0	10.2
Red River	15	6.1	6.1
Arkansas River	11	4.5	5.8

[1] Distribution based on 462 counties. The counties with no plantations included in the matched series for 1937 and 1934 were omitted. See table A.

WPA Form DRS 200A

WORKS PROGRESS ADMINISTRATION

Harry L. Hopkins, Administrator

PLANTATION SCHEDULE

Enumerated by _____ Edited by (1) _____ (2) _____
1. Operator's name _____ Same as 1934 _____ Tract number _____
2. Location of plantation: State _____ County _____ Township _____
   Road _____ Nearest town _____ Distance (miles from) _____
3. Operator's residence: On plantation _____ Miles away _____ Address _____
4. How many other farms owned _____ 5. Other occupation of operator _____
6. Acres operated:

Item	1934	1935	1936	1937	1938
Total owned					
Additional rented					
Plantation total					
Rented out					

7. Value: Of farm land ____ Of operator's residence ____ Other buildings ____
   Animals _____ Machinery _____ Total value _____
8. Number of vacant houses which are habitable or could be made so for $50 ___
9. Type of tenant—1938:   10. Type of land:

Item	Acres operated	Number of families
Wage hand		
Cropper		
Share tenant		
Renter (cash or standing)		
Family in house without crop		
Total		

Item	Acres
In crops	
Tillable land idle	
Pasture	
Woods not pastured	
Waste land	
Total	

Farm Year Beginning 1937

11. Crop record:

Crop	Har-vested acres	Quantity produced	Operator's sales			Total tenant shares
			Price	Quantity	Value	
1. Cotton, wage						
2. Cottonseed, wage						
3. Cotton, cropper						
4. Cottonseed, cropper						
5. Cotton, share tenant						
6. Cottonseed, share tenant						
7. Corn, wage						
8. Corn fodder, wage						
9. Corn, cropper						
10. Corn fodder, cropper						
11. Corn, share tenant						
12. Corn fodder, share tenant						
13. Tobacco, wage						
14. Tobacco, cropper						
15. Tobacco, share tenant						
16. Irish potatoes						
17. Sweet potatoes						
18. Wheat						
19. Oats						
20. Cowpeas for seed						
21. Cowpeas for hay						
22. Alfalfa hay						
23. Peanuts						
24. Sugar cane						
25. Sorghum						
26. Soy beans						
27. Oats, clover, vetch						
28. Other (specify)						
29.						
30.						
31.						
32. Orchard						
33. Garden						
34. Total crops						
35. Other sources of income, rent received						
36. Charges against tenant shares						
37. Other (specify)						
Total						

12. A. A. A.—soil conservation bene-
    fits:

To landlord (1937 crop)_____
To tenant (1937 crop)_____

13. Livestock products:

Item	Operator's sales		
	Price	Quan-tity	Value
Butter_____	_____	_____	_____
Milk_____	_____	_____	_____
Chickens_____	_____	_____	_____
Eggs_____	_____	_____	_____
Pork and pork products__	_____	_____	_____
Beef_____	_____	_____	_____
Total_____	_____	_____	_____

14. Total cash income:
    (11, 12, 13)_____

16. Livestock (plantation owned):

Horses_____
Mules_____
Cows_____
Calves_____
Sheep or goats_____
Pigs_____
Chickens_____
Other_____
Number of above work stock kept in central barn
  or pastures_____
Number kept on tenant acres_____
What items of feed   Why_____
were bought
_____   _____
_____   _____
_____   _____
_____   _____

15. Current expenses:

Item	Total amount
Wage hands_____	_____
Rations or board_____	_____
Cotton chopping_____	_____
Cotton picking_____	_____
Miscellaneous labor_____	_____
Tenant occasional labor_____	_____
Repairs, dwelling_____	_____
Repairs, barns, fences, implements_____	_____
Feed, grain_____	_____
Feed, roughage_____	_____
Veterinary fees, etc_____	_____
Seeds, etc_____	_____
Fertilizer, wages_____	_____
Fertilizer, soda, tenant and cropper____	_____
Insurance on property_____	_____
Taxes_____	_____
Rent_____	_____
Interest_____	_____
Ginning_____	_____
Total expenses_____	_____

Cash after settling, to tenants_____
Total tenants' share of expenses_____

17.

Number of families advanced subsistence_____
Usual monthly advance____   Number of months___
Total landlord advances for subsistence_____
Interest rate charged_____
Amount of interest_____

18. Number of tenant and laborer families living on place and size of operations:

Item	1938		1937		1936		1935		1934	
	White	Negro	White	Negro	White	Negro	White	Negro	White	Negro
Total families										
Wage hand										
Cropper										
Share tenant										
Renter										
Displaced										
Land in crops										

18a. Seasonal labor:

(1) Percent of operator cotton chopped with off-plantation labor_____
(2) Percent of renter cotton chopped with off-plantation labor_____
(3) Percent of share renter cotton chopped with off-plantation labor_____
(4) Percent of cropper cotton chopped with off-plantation labor_____
(5) Percent of operator cotton picked with off-plantation labor_____
(6) Percent of renter cotton picked with off-plantation labor_____
(7) Percent of share renter cotton picked with off-plantation labor_____
(8) Percent of cropper cotton picked with off-plantation labor_____

18b. Number of families who started to share crop in 1937 but who "gave up
    their crop"_____
    Why_____

18c. Reasons for changes in labor utilization since 1934:

Changes	Reasons
1934–35	
1935–36	
1936–37	
1937–38	

18d. Availability of types of labor in 1937:

Type of labor	Plenti-ful	Scarce	Suffi-cient	Explanations
Tenant				
Share tenant				
Cropper				
Wage family				
Wage hand				
Nonresident seasonal labor				

19. Landlord borrowing for current expenses in 1937:

Source	Time used		Interest paid	Security	Amount
	Date borrowed	Date repaid			
Bank					
Fertilizer company					
Merchant					
Government					
Total					

20. Landlord debts (excluding those for current crop):

Type	December 31, 1936		December 31, 1937	
	Amount	Rate	Amount	Rate
Mortgage:				
Land				
Chattels				
Bank				
Merchant note				
Open account				
Government				
Other				

21. What principal changes in the cropping and other farm enterprises have taken place since 1934?

Changes with respect to—	Reasons for change
Cotton:	
1935	
1936	
1937	
1938	
Corn:	
1935	
1936	
1937	
1938	
Conservation crops:	
1935	
1936	
1937	
1938	
Beef cattle:	
1935	
1936	
1937	
1938	
Dairy:	
1935	
1936	
1937	
1938	
Hogs:	
1935	
1936	
1937	
1938	
Fruits and vegetables:	
1935	
1936	
1937	
1938	
Other (specify):	
1935	
1936	
1937	
1938	

22. How are the changes in the cropping and other farm enterprises related to changes in labor utilization? _____

_____

23. What effect have the changes in the cropping and other farm enterprises had on the well-being of croppers and laborers remaining on the farm?

_____

24. Trend in mechanization of farm operations:

A. Tractors	Year started	Kind	Model	Capacity	Number of tractors				
					1938	1937	1936	1935	1934

B. Amount of multiple row equipment	Year started	Type	Number of rows or size	Number of each type				
				1938	1937	1936	1935	1934
1. Tractor:								
2. Four-horse:								
3. Three-horse:								
4. Two-horse:								
5. One-horse:								

				1938	1937	1936	1935	1934
C.		Acres handled by tractors hired from others						

25. Acres handled in 1937 by power and workstock combinations:

Item	Four-row tractor		Two-row tractor		Four-horse		Three-horse		Two-horse		One-horse	
	Acres	Year started	Acres	Year started	Acres	Year started	Acres	Year started	Acres	Year started	Acres	Year started
Breaking												
Seedbed preparation												
Planting												
Cultivating												
Mowing												

26. (a) How many work stock have been displaced by the tractors used in 1937?_____ Explain_____

(b) Could further reductions have been made in 1937? Yes ( ) No ( ); Number of work stock _____ Explain_____

(c) Could further reductions have been made in 1938? Yes ( ) No ( ); Number of work stock _____ Explain_____

27. (a) Were reductions in the number of resident cropper and wage families made by the use of tractors in 1937? Yes ( ) No ( ). If yes, how many families were eliminated? _____ Explain_____

(b) Could further reductions have been made? Yes ( ) No ( ); Number of families _____ Explain_____

28. What factors retard the shift to greater mechanization on the farm? List:
_____
_____
_____
_____

29. Arrangements with respect to 1937 nonresident seasonal labor:

Item	Cotton pickers	Cotton choppers
1. Source		
2. Who furnished transportation		
Cost of transportation		
3. Miles to obtain:		
Total		
Over hard surface road		
Over dirt road		
4. Accommodations furnished:		
Shelter		
Board		
Other		

Remarks: _____

_____

_____

Appendix D

CHANGES IN LABOR REQUIREMENTS FOR COTTON PRODUCTION

FOR THE purpose of estimating changes in the amount of labor used in producing cotton in the United States, the cotton-producing States were divided into five selected areas: Southeastern cotton, other Southeastern, Southwestern, California, and all other States.[1]

In calculating the amount of labor required for cotton production, the man-hours per acre for each State were weighted by harvested acreage to obtain a rate for each area [2] (table C). The average man-hours for each area were then weighted by the respective acreage to give the average man-hours per acre for the United States. For the crop year 1938 an average of 106 man-hours of labor was used per acre actually harvested in the United States. Labor requirements fluctuate from year to year, however, as the estimated amount of labor used annually in producing cotton varies directly with acreage harvested and yield per acre [3] (table D).

The amount of labor required to produce an acre of cotton rose steadily from 1934 to 1937 and then declined in 1938. This increase

---

[1] The Southeastern cotton area includes Alabama, Arkansas, Georgia, Louisiana, Mississippi, North Carolina, and South Carolina. The other Southeastern area includes Florida, Tennessee, and Virginia. The Southwestern area includes Arizona, New Mexico, Oklahoma, and Texas. All other States include Illinois, Kansas, Kentucky, and Missouri.

[2] See Holley, William C. and Arnold, Lloyd E., *Changes in Technology and Labor Requirements in Crop Production: Cotton*, Report No. A–7, National Research Project, Works Progress Administration, Philadelphia, Pa., September 1938, pp. 124–127.

[3] Basic factors affecting yield per acre from year to year are deficient and/or excessive moisture, insect damages, plant diseases, and losses from frost, floods, excessive heat, and hot winds.

in labor was related to the yield of lint per acre which also rose annually from 1934 to 1937, followed by a decrease in 1938. The average labor per bale [4] for the United States amounted to 213 man-hours in 1937 as compared with 217 man-hours in 1934 but rose to 215 man-hours in 1938.

Table C.—Estimated Labor Requirements for Cotton Production in the United States per Acre and per Bale, by Area and State, 1934–1938

| Area and State | Man-hours [1] | | | | | | | | | | | | | | |
| | Total (in millions) | | | | | Per acre | | | | | Per bale (500 pounds gross weight) | | | | |
	1938	1937	1936	1935	1934	1938	1937	1936	1935	1934	1938	1937	1936	1935	1934
United States total	2,564	4,044	2,700	2,294	2,090	106	120	91	83	78	215	213	218	216	217
Southeastern cotton States	1,635	2,593	1,856	1,488	1,389	137	163	134	122	112	244	244	244	244	243
Alabama	272	412	288	267	239	132	153	124	119	112	252	253	252	252	252
Arkansas	325	459	311	205	208	153	165	125	96	96	241	241	240	240	239
Georgia	211	370	269	261	238	105	139	118	121	111	248	247	248	246	246
Louisiana	171	279	193	141	122	153	178	138	111	103	253	253	254	254	252
Mississippi	413	653	465	307	278	163	191	155	112	110	242	243	243	244	243
North Carolina	86	173	133	127	141	100	157	139	137	145	222	222	223	222	223
South Carolina	157	247	197	180	163	126	146	141	132	127	242	241	241	242	240
Other Southeastern States	144	201	134	101	126	169	179	143	114	138	273	270	270	267	269
Florida	9	13	11	10	9	115	114	120	116	102	346	325	355	323	321
Virginia	3	9	7	6	8	66	137	131	120	133	250	209	212	200	222
Tennessee	132	179	116	85	109	180	190	146	113	143	269	269	268	268	269
Southwestern States	673	1,089	601	644	499	63	71	42	49	38	171	170	170	173	170
Arizona	31	49	30	21	18	152	165	144	133	135	158	157	157	156	154
New Mexico	13	23	16	11	13	143	144	134	117	141	135	141	144	147	144
Oklahoma	111	152	56	111	64	67	64	25	48	24	197	197	193	196	199
Texas	518	865	499	501	404	59	69	43	47	40	168	168	170	169	168
California	48	83	50	27	29	141	134	135	124	131	113	112	113	113	112
All other States [2]	64	78	59	34	47	170	132	135	99	134	182	183	182	183	184

[1] Based on harvested acreage.
[2] Illinois, Kansas, Kentucky, and Missouri.

Source: Based on data from the U. S. Department of Agriculture, Bureau of Agricultural Economics, Washington, D. C.

In the Southeastern cotton area an average of 137 man-hours was utilized in producing an acre of cotton for the year 1938, or 31 hours more than the average for the United States. The high labor requirements resulted largely from small cotton acreages per farm, the use of small horse-drawn equipment, the large amounts of fertilizer applied, high yields, and the great amount of labor used in hoeing, chopping, and harvesting. In 1937 which was a year of much higher yields than 1938 the average amount of labor per acre in the Southeastern cotton area was 163 man-hours.

More labor was used in 1938 in the other Southeastern States and all other States than in the remaining sections of the United States in which cotton is raised. This is explained by the small cotton acreages and large amounts of hand labor used.

In terms of man-hours per bale of cotton produced also, more labor was used in the Southeastern cotton States and other Southeastern

[4] 500 pounds gross weight (includes bagging and ties and contains an average of 478 pounds of lint).

Table D.—Cotton Acres Harvested, Production, and Yield, by Area and State, 1934-1938

Area and State	Acres harvested (in thousands)					Bales [1] produced (in thousands)					Yield of lint per acre (pounds)				
	1938	1937	1936	1935	1934	1938	1937	1936	1935	1934	1938	1937	1936	1935	1934
United States total	24,248	33,623	29,755	27,509	26,866	11,943	18,946	12,399	10,638	9,636	236	270	199	185	172
Southeastern cotton States	11,944	15,925	13,842	12,835	12,417	6,698	10,634	7,611	6,102	5,723	268	319	263	238	220
Alabama	2,058	2,694	2,321	2,243	2,133	1,081	1,631	1,145	1,059	950	251	290	236	226	213
Arkansas	2,125	2,782	2,490	2,137	2,167	1,349	1,904	1,295	853	869	304	328	249	191	192
Georgia	2,009	2,661	2,276	2,155	2,142	852	1,500	1,086	1,059	968	203	270	228	235	216
Louisiana	1,119	1,569	1,401	1,268	1,189	676	1,104	761	556	485	289	337	260	210	195
Mississippi	2,533	3,421	2,998	2,740	2,530	1,704	2,692	1,911	1,259	1,142	322	377	305	220	216
North Carolina	857	1,103	957	930	970	388	780	597	572	631	216	338	298	294	311
South Carolina	1,243	1,695	1,399	1,362	1,286	648	1,023	816	744	678	249	289	279	261	252
Other Southeastern States	849	1,121	938	891	908	528	744	497	378	469	297	317	253	203	247
Florida	76	118	88	89	92	26	40	31	31	28	163	162	170	165	145
Tennessee	733	937	797	750	759	490	661	433	317	405	320	338	260	202	255
Virginia	40	66	53	52	57	12	43	33	30	36	149	312	298	273	302
Southwestern States	10,737	15,369	14,172	13,225	12,970	3,941	6,403	3,525	3,733	2,929	175	199	119	135	108
Arizona	203	299	208	160	136	196	313	191	135	117	462	501	438	405	410
New Mexico	94	159	116	90	90	96	163	111	75	90	489	490	457	398	480
Oklahoma	1,656	2,372	2,251	2,318	2,647	563	773	290	567	321	163	156	62	117	58
Texas	8,784	12,539	11,597	10,657	10,097	3,086	5,154	2,933	2,956	2,401	168	197	121	133	114
California	341	620	368	218	223	424	738	442	239	259	594	569	574	524	555
All other States [2]	377	588	435	340	348	352	427	324	186	256	446	347	356	261	352

[1] 500 pounds gross weight.
[2] Illinois, Kansas, Kentucky, and Missouri.

Source: Based on data from the U. S. Department of Agriculture, Bureau of Agricultural Economics, Washington, D. C.

States than elsewhere. During the crop year 1938 this amounted to 244 and 273 man-hours, respectively. Since 1934, however, the man-hours required per bale have remained practically constant for both areas.

Less labor was used per acre of cotton in the Southwestern States than in other areas. In 1938 the average was only 63 man-hours per acre or 43 hours less than the average for the United States. This difference was due to the use of large-scale equipment, less hand labor, and fewer operations, as well as smaller yields which required less labor to harvest. On the basis of labor per bale, however, the advantage of the Southwestern area is much less than it is on the basis of labor per acre. In 1937, 170 man-hours were used per bale as compared with 213 man-hours for the United States.

California has relatively high labor requirements for irrigation, hoeing, chopping, and harvesting. The latter requires large amounts of hand labor because of exceptionally high yields per acre. An increase from 1934 to 1938 of 10 hours per acre in labor required was due to increased yields. No change was noted in average man-hours per bale.

In 1938 approximately 2.6 billion hours of labor were used in producing cotton in the United States. This estimate is about one and one-half billion hours below that for 1937 and approximately one-half billion hours greater than the amount of labor used in 1934. Considerably more than 50 percent of the total labor used for cotton production in each year from 1934 through 1938 was in the Southeastern cotton States. The Southwestern States were next in importance, accounting for approximately one-fourth of all labor requirements.

Index

INDEX

	Page
Absentee ownership	2
Acreage. *See* Crop acreage; Idle cropland.	
Agricultural Adjustment Administration	3, 5, 10, 29, 31, 32, 40
Almack, R. B.	68n
Areas surveyed (*see also* Plantations surveyed)	xi–xiii, 103
Arnold, Lloyd E	115n
Bankhead Cotton Act	3
Bennett, Charles A	22n
Blalock, H. W	58n
Burney, L. E	61n
Caliver, Ambrose	66n, 96n
Cash renter, definition of	7
Census, Bureau of the:	
Agriculture	48n, 49n
Mortality Statistics	60n, 61n
Civil Works Administration	51–52, 61
Clark, Taliaferro	61n
Compulsory school attendance	66
Cook, Katherine M	66n
Cotton yield, factors affecting	9–10, 81
Credit, short-term:	
Of operators	24–26, 86
Of tenants	26–28
Crop acreage:	
By tenure and crop	6–9
In corn	5, 80
In cotton	5, 80–81
In peanuts	5, 80
In tobacco	5, 80
Trend in	3–4, 79
Crop year, special factors affecting	xi, 5
Cropper, definition of	7
Debts, long-term, of operators	23–24, 85
Dickens, Dorothy	57n
Diet, adequacy of	55–58

Education (*see also* Illiteracy):   *Page*
    One-room and two-room schools _ _ _ _ _ _ _ _ _ _ _ _ _ _ _ _ _   66
    School attainment _ 64–65
    Special handicaps to   _ _ _ _ _ _ _ _ _ _ _ _ _ _ _ _ _ _ _ 64–65, 96
    Support of _   63
Edwards, Newton _   63n
Electrical service _ 68–69
Embree, Edwin R _   67n
Ensminger, Douglas _   58n
Expenses, current:
    Operator _ 40–41, 95
    Plantation _ 34–35, 92, 93
    Tenant _   44

Farm operators, changes in, by tenure _ _ _ _ _ _ _ _ _ _ _ _ _ _ _   49
Farm Security Administration _ _ _ _ _ _ _ _ _ _ _ _ 51–53, 62, 73, 74, 75
Federal aid per capita _ 51–52
Federal Emergency Relief Administration _ _ _ _ _ _ _ _ _ _ 51–52, 61, 63
Federal Housing Authority _   75

Gregory, Cecil L _   58n

Hamilton, C. Horace _   18n
Health conditions (*see also* Infant mortality; names of specific diseases) _ _ 60–62
Holley, William C _   115n
Horne, Roman L _   21n
Hospital facilities _   62
Housing, farm _ 58–59

Idle cropland _   3–4
Illiteracy _ 63–64
Income:
    Cropper _   51
    Operator:
        Gross cash _ 39–40, 94, 95
        Net cash _ 41–43, 94, 95
    Plantation:
        For highest and lowest one-fourth _ _ _ _ _ _ _ _ _ _ _ 33–34, 91
        Gross _ _ _ _ _ _ _ _ _ _ _ _ _ _ _ _ _ _ 30–34, 89, 90, 93
        Net cash _ 35–37, 93
    Tenant:
        Gross cash _ 43–44
        Net _   46
        Net cash _ 45–46, 96
Infant mortality _   61
Interest, annual rates of _ _ _ _ _ _ _ _ _ _ _ _ _ 24, 25, 27–28, 85, 86, 87
Investment, plantation, by type _ _ _ _ _ _ _ _ _ _ _ _ _ _ _ _ 29–30, 88

Johnson, E. A _   22

Labor:
    By type _ 13–15, 81–83
    Distribution of, by tenure _ _ _ _ _ _ _ _ _ _ _ _ _ _ _ _ _ _ _   7–8

Labor—Continued.
    Off-plantation: *Page*
        By type _ 16
        Extent of_ 15–16
        Transportation of _ 17, 84
Labor requirements for cotton production, by area and State_ _ _ _ _ 115–118
Langsford, E. L_ 20n, 26n
Library facilities _ 69, 97
Lively, C. E _ 68n
Livestock, increase in (*see also* Work stock) _ _ _ _ _ _ _ _ _ _ _ 10–11

McKibben, Eugene G _ 21n
Magazine circulation _ 69, 97
Malaria _ 61
Mangus, A. R _ _ _ _ _ _ _ _ _ _ _ _ _ _ _ _ _ _ _ 61n, 65n, 68n
Mechanization:
    Extent of _ 17–20, 84
    Increases in _ 20–22
Medical care program, of Farm Security Administration _ _ _ _ _ _ _ 62
Migration. *See* Population, farm.
Moser, Ada M _ 56n

National Emergency Council _ _ _ _ _ _ _ _ _ _ _ _ _ _ _ _ _ _ 76n
Need, extent of _ _ _ _ _ _ _ _ _ _ _ _ _ _ _ _ _ _ 50–51, 53–54
Negro tenants _ 15

Office of Education. *See* U. S. Department of the Interior.

Pellagra _ 60–61
Plane-of-living index_ 67–68
Plantation, definition of _ _ _ _ _ _ _ _ _ _ _ _ _ _ _ _ _ _ xi, 103
Plantation operator:
    Duties of_ 1
    Second occupation_ 1–2
Plantations surveyed _ _ _ _ _ _ _ _ _ _ _ _ _ _ _ xi–xii, 103–105
Population, farm:
    Changes in _ 48–49
    Migration of _ 48
*Proceedings of the National Health Conference_* _ _ _ _ _ _ _ _ _ _ _ 62
Production, home-use _ _ _ _ _ _ _ _ _ _ _ _ _ _ _ _ _ 39n, 46, 58

Recommendations for improving Southern rural conditions _ _ _ _ _ 72–76
Relief, general _ 53
Relief loads _ 52–53
Resettlement Administration _ _ _ _ _ _ _ _ _ _ _ _ _ _ _ _ _ 51–53
Resident families, by type _ _ _ _ _ _ _ _ _ _ _ _ _ 13–15, 81–83
Rural Electrification Administration _ _ _ _ _ _ _ _ _ _ _ _ _ _ _ 68n

Sample:
    Distribution of _ 104–105
    Representativeness of _ _ _ _ _ _ _ _ _ _ _ _ _ _ _ _ _ _ 104
Schedule _ 106–114

Page

Sebrell, W. H. _   61n
Share tenant, definition of _   7
Size of plantations_   3–4
Smith, T. Lynn _   64n
Soil Conservation Service _ 72–73
Standing renter, definition of _ _ _ _ _ _ _ _ _ _ _ _ _ _ _ _ _ _ _   7
Study of Consumer Purchases _ _ _ _ _ _ _ _ _ _ _ _ _ _ _ _ _ _   59
Subsistence advances _ _ _ _ _ _ _ _ _ _ _ _ _ _ _ _ 26–28, 44, 51, 56, 87
Survey, scope of _   103

Tandy, Elizabeth C _   62n
Technical Committee on Medical Care_ _ _ _ _ _ _ _ _ _ _ _ _ _ _ _   60n
Thibodeaux, B. H _ 20n, 26n
Tractors, use of _ 17–20, 84
Turner, H. A _   49n
Typhoid and paratyphoid fever _ _ _ _ _ _ _ _ _ _ _ _ _ _ _ _ _ _ _   60

Unemployment Census, November 1937 _ _ _ _ _ _ _ _ _ _ _ _ _ _ _   50
U. S. Department of Agriculture:
    Agricultural situation, summary _ _ _ _ _ _ _ _ _ _ _ _ _ _ _ _   87n
    Data on cotton production _ _ _ _ _ _ _ _ _ _ _ _ _ _ _ _ 116, 117
    Farm housing data _   59n
    Farm population estimates _ _ _ _ _ _ _ _ _ _ _ _ _ _ _ _ _ _   48n
U. S. Department of the Interior, Office of Education _ _ _ _ _ _ _ _   63n
United States Housing Authority _ _ _ _ _ _ _ _ _ _ _ _ _ _ _ _ 76–76

Veneral disease _   61

Wage hand, definition of _   7n
Whetten, Nathan L _   65n
White, H. C _   56n
White, Max R _   58n
Williams, R. C _   62n
Wilson, Louis R_   97n
Woofter, T. J., Jr _ _ _ _ _ _ _ _ _ _ _ xin, 1n, 5n, 50n, 58n, 63n, 72n, 103n
Work Projects Administration _ _ _ _ _ _ _ _ _ _ _ _ _ _ 51–53, 61, 63, 75
Work stock, changes in use of (*see also* Livestock) _ _ _ _ _ _ _ _ 17–20, 84

Zimmerman, Carle C _   65n